Standard Grade | Credit

Chemistry

Credit Level 2003

Credit Level 2004

Credit Level 2005

Credit Level 2006

Credit Level 2007

Leckie × Leckie

First exam published in 2003.
Published by Leckie & Leckie Ltd, 3rd Floor, 4 Queen Street, Edinburgh EH2 1JE
tel: 0131 220 6831 fax: 0131 225 9987 enquiries@leckieandleckie.co.uk www.leckieandleckie.co.uk

ISBN 978-1-84372-504-6

A CIP Catalogue record for this book is available from the British Library.

Printed in Scotland by Scotprint.

Leckie & Leckie is a division of Huveaux plc.

Leckie & Leckie is grateful to the copyright holders, as credited at the back of the book, for permission to use their material. Every effort has been made to trace the copyright holders and to obtain their permission for the use of copyright material. Leckie & Leckie will gladly receive information enabling them to rectify any error or omission in subsequent editions.

2003 | Credit

[BLANK PAGE]

FOR OFFICIAL USE

C

	KU	PS
Total Marks		

0500/402

NATIONAL QUALIFICATIONS 2003

FRIDAY, 23 MAY
10.50 AM – 12.20 PM

CHEMISTRY
STANDARD GRADE
Credit Level

Fill in these boxes and read what is printed below.

Full name of centre

Town

Forename(s)

Surname

Date of birth
Day Month Year

Scottish candidate number

Number of seat

1 All questions should be attempted.

2 Necessary data will be found in the Data Booklet provided for Chemistry at Standard Grade and Intermediate 2.

3 The questions may be answered in any order but all answers are to be written in this answer book, and must be written clearly and legibly in ink.

4 Rough work, if any should be necessary, as well as the fair copy, is to be written in this book.

Rough work should be scored through when the fair copy has been written.

5 Additional space for answers and rough work will be found at the end of the book.

6 The size of the space provided for an answer should not be taken as an indication of how much to write. It is not necessary to use all the space.

7 Before leaving the examination room you must give this book to the invigilator. If you do not, you may lose all the marks for this paper.

SCOTTISH QUALIFICATIONS AUTHORITY

SAB 0500/402 6/27120

PART 1

In Questions 1 to 9 of this part of the paper, an answer is given by circling the appropriate letter (or letters) in the answer grid provided.

In some questions, two letters are required for full marks.

If more than the correct number of answers is given, marks will be deducted.

In some cases, the number of correct responses is NOT identified in the question.

A total of 20 marks is available in this part of the paper.

SAMPLE QUESTION

A CH_4	B H_2	C CO_2
D CO	E C_2H_5OH	F C

(*a*) Identify the hydrocarbon(s).

(A)	B	C
D	E	F

The one correct answer to part (*a*) is A. This should be circled.

(*b*) Identify the **two** elements.

A	(B)	C
D	E	(F)

As indicated in this question, there are **two** correct answers to part (*b*). These are B and F. Both answers are circled.

(*c*) Identify the substance(s) which can burn to produce **both** carbon dioxide and water.

(A)	B	C
D	(E)	F

There are **two** correct answers to part (*c*). These are A and E.

Both answers are circled.

If, after you have recorded your answer, you decide that you have made an error and wish to make a change, you should cancel the original answer and circle the answer you now consider to be correct. Thus, in part (*a*), if you want to change an answer A to an answer D, your answer sheet would look like this:

~~(A)~~	B	C
(D)	E	F

If you want to change back to an answer which has already been scored out, you should enter a tick (✓) in the box of the answer of your choice, thus:

✓ ~~(A)~~	B	C
~~(D)~~	E	F

DO NOT WRITE IN THIS MARGIN

KU PS

1. Atoms are made up of protons, neutrons and electrons.

A	The number of protons
B	The number of neutrons
C	The number of electrons
D	The number of outer electrons
E	The number of protons plus neutrons

(*a*) Identify the **two** numbers which are the same in a neutral atom.

A
B
C
D
E

(*b*) Identify the mass number of an atom.

A
B
C
D
E

[Turn over

DO NOT WRITE IN THIS MARGIN

KU	PS

2. The names of several compounds are shown in the grid.

A potassium nitrate	B sodium hydroxide	C lithium sulphate
D aluminium chloride	E ammonium phosphate	F calcium chloride

(*a*) Identify the **two** compounds which can be used as fertilisers.

A	B	C
D	E	F

(*b*) Identify the **two** compounds which react together to produce ammonia.

A	B	C
D	E	F

DO NOT WRITE IN THIS MARGIN

KU PS

3. Hydrocarbons are compounds made from hydrogen and carbon only.

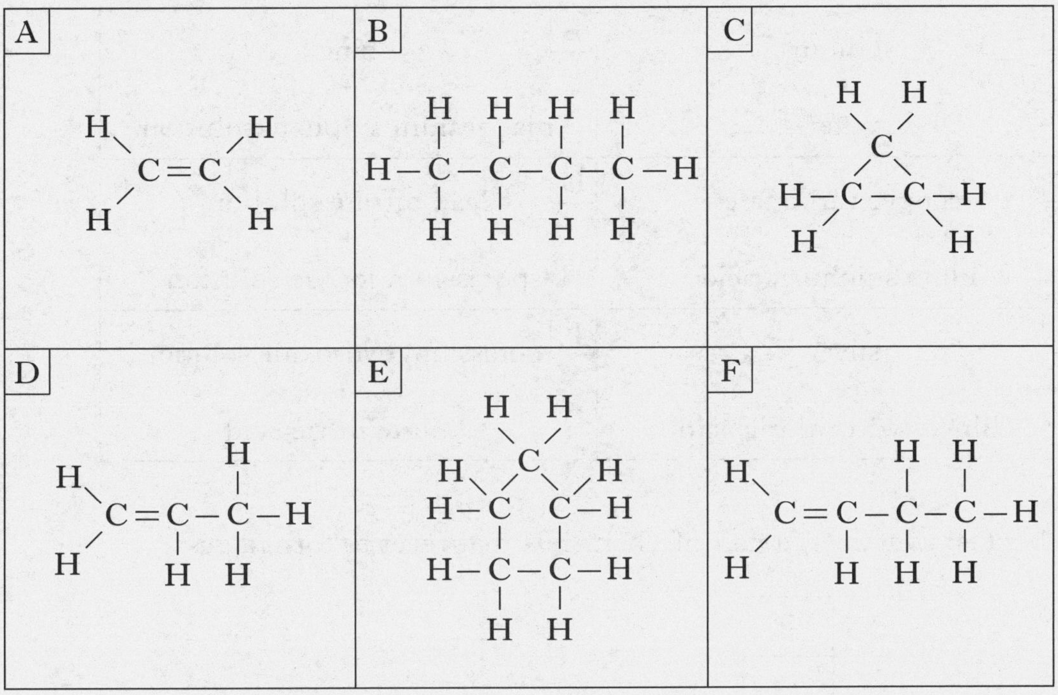

(*a*) Identify the hydrocarbon which reacts with hydrogen to form butane.

A	B	C
D	E	F

(*b*) Identify the **two** isomers.

A	B	C
D	E	F

(*c*) Identify the hydrocarbon(s) which is (are) the first member(s) of a homologous series.

A	B	C
D	E	F

[Turn over

DO NOT WRITE IN THIS MARGIN

KU	PS

4. The grid shows some pairs of chemicals.

A sodium + water	B zinc + magnesium sulphate solution
C copper carbonate + dilute sulphuric acid	D lead nitrate solution + potassium iodide solution
E silver + dilute hydrochloric acid	F potassium hydroxide solution + dilute nitric acid

Which box(es) contain(s) a pair of chemicals that react to form a gas?

A	B
C	D
E	F

DO NOT WRITE IN THIS MARGIN

KU PS

5. Identify the result(s) obtained in the reaction between dilute sulphuric acid and barium hydroxide solution.

You may wish to use the data booklet to help you.

A	The pH of the acid went down.
B	Carbon dioxide was produced.
C	A precipitate was formed.
D	Hydrogen was produced.
E	Water was produced.

A
B
C
D
E

[Turn over

DO NOT WRITE IN THIS MARGIN

KU	PS

6. Oil rigs made from iron should be protected from rusting.

Identify the correct statement(s).

A	Salt water slows down rusting.
B	Tin gives sacrificial protection to the iron.
C	The rusting of iron is an example of oxidation.
D	Ferroxyl indicator turns blue in the presence of Fe^{2+} ions.
E	Iron rusts faster when connected to the negative terminal of a battery.

A
B
C
D
E

DO NOT WRITE IN THIS MARGIN

KU	PS

7. Iron(III) oxide is an ionic compound.

Identify the correct statement(s).

A	It is a salt.
B	It can be reduced to iron.
C	It has the formula Fe_2O_3.
D	It is made up of molecules.
E	It does not react with acid.

A
B
C
D
E

[Turn over

DO NOT WRITE IN THIS MARGIN

KU	PS

8. The table contains information about some solid, liquid and gaseous compounds.

Compound	**Melting point /°C**	**Boiling point /°C**	**pH of solution in water**
A	319	1390	11
B	801	1413	7
C	−115	−85	3
D	−93	−6	11
E	−95	56	7
F	63	189	3

(*a*) Identify the compound which is a gas at 25 °C and forms an acidic solution.

A
B
C
D
E
F

(*b*) Identify the compound which could be sodium hydroxide.

A
B
C
D
E
F

DO NOT WRITE IN THIS MARGIN

KU	PS

9. Substances can be classified as conductors or non-conductors and also as solids or liquids.

Substance	State	Conductor or non-conductor
A	solid	non-conductor
B	liquid	non-conductor
C	solid	conductor
D	liquid	conductor

(*a*) Which **two** substances could be sodium chloride?

A
B
C
D

(*b*) Which substance could **not** be a compound?

A
B
C
D

[Turn over

DO NOT WRITE IN THIS MARGIN

Marks | KU | PS

PART 2

A total of 40 marks is available in this part of the paper.

10. The diagrams show how different flames can be produced in a Bunsen burner.

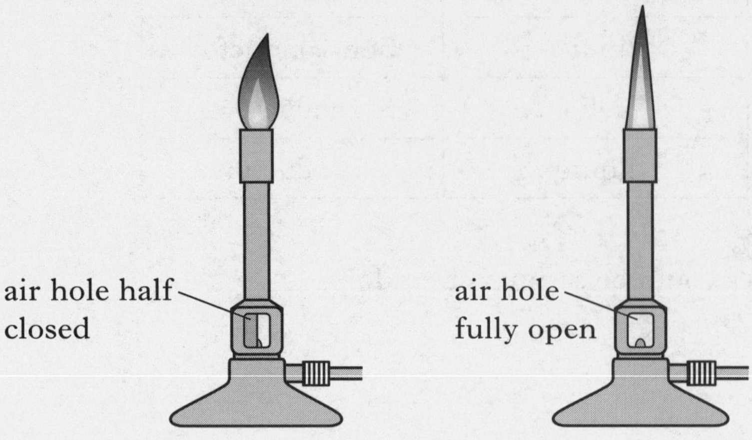

(*a*) The fuel used in a Bunsen burner is methane, CH_4.
What is meant by the term "fuel"?

____

____ **1**

(*b*) Methane burns to form carbon dioxide and water.

(i) Balance this equation.

$$CH_4 \quad + \quad O_2 \quad \rightarrow \quad CO_2 \quad + \quad H_2O$$

1

(ii) Name another product which could be formed in Flame **A**.

____ **1**

(*c*) Draw a diagram to show the **shape** of a methane molecule.

1

(4)

DO NOT WRITE IN THIS MARGIN

Marks KU PS

11. There are two different types of chlorine atom: $^{35}_{17}Cl$ and $^{37}_{17}Cl$.

(*a*) (i) What name is used to describe these different types of chlorine atom?

______________________________ **1**

(ii) A natural sample of chlorine has an average atomic mass of 35·5.

What is the mass number of the more abundant type of chlorine atom in the sample?

______________________________ **1**

(*b*) The atoms in a chlorine molecule are held together by a covalent bond.
A covalent bond is a shared pair of electrons.

Explain how this holds the atoms together.

____

____

____

____

______________________________ **1**

(*c*) Complete the table to show the number of each type of particle in a $^{35}_{17}Cl^{-}$ ion.

Particle	**Number**
proton	
neutron	
electron	

2

(5)

[Turn over

DO NOT WRITE IN THIS MARGIN

Marks KU PS

12. Hydrogen can be produced in the laboratory by adding excess hydrochloric acid to lumps of zinc. The reaction stops when all the zinc is used up.

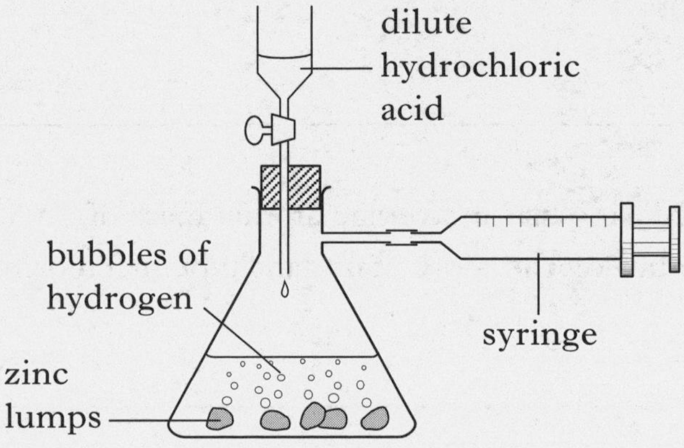

The volume of hydrogen gas produced over a period of time was measured and the results are shown in the table.

Time/s	0	20	40	60	80	100	120	140
Volume of hydrogen/cm^3	0	30	51	65	74	78	80	80

(*a*) Draw a line graph of the results.

Use appropriate scales to fill most of the graph paper.

(Additional graph paper, if required, will be found on page 24.)

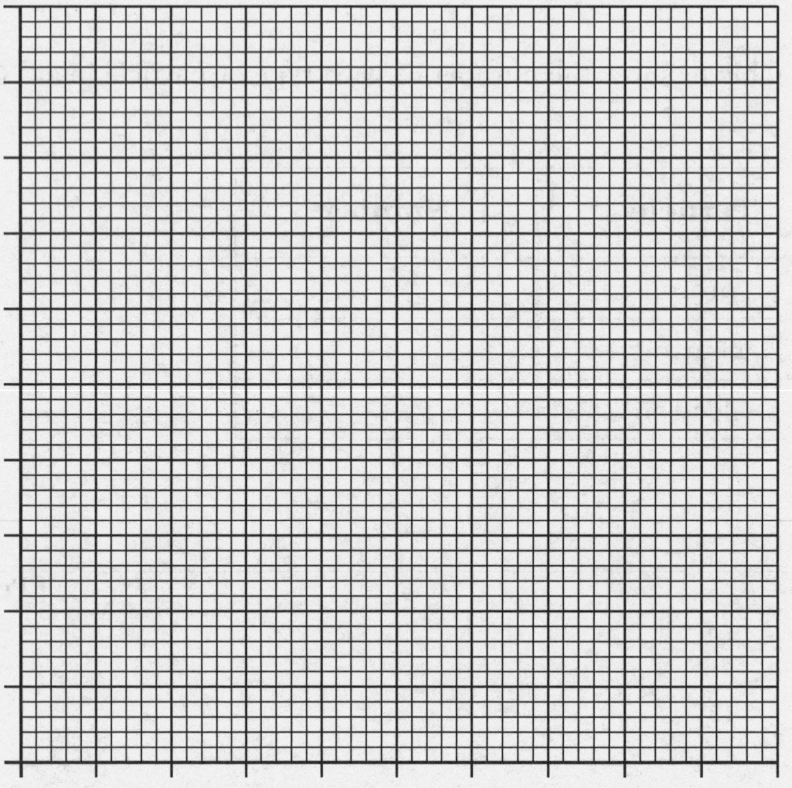

2

DO NOT WRITE IN THIS MARGIN

Marks | KU | PS

12. (continued)

(*b*) Use your graph to estimate the time, in seconds, for 40 cm^3 of hydrogen to be produced.

____ **1**

(*c*) The equation for the reaction of zinc with hydrochloric acid is

$$Zn + 2HCl \rightarrow ZnCl_2 + H_2$$

Calculate the mass of zinc required to produce 0·5 mole of hydrogen.

Answer: ____________ g **1**

(4)

[Turn over

DO NOT WRITE IN THIS MARGIN

Marks KU PS

13. Mrs Smith gave her class three chemicals labelled **P**, **Q** and **R**.

The chemicals were ethanol (C_2H_5OH) solution, silver nitrate solution and dilute sulphuric acid.

The class used the following apparatus to identify each solution.

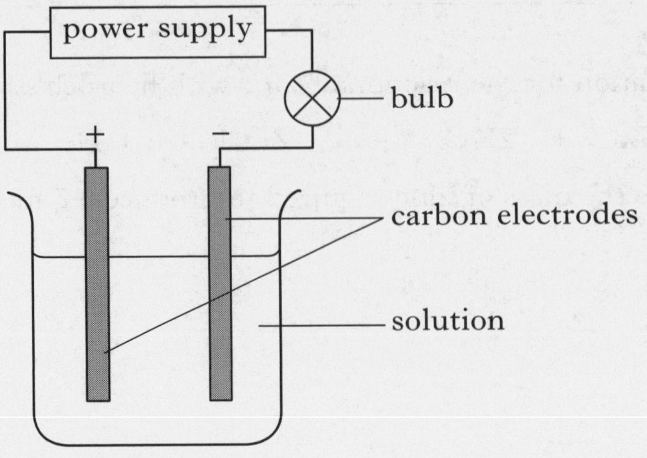

The results are shown in the table.

Solution	Bulb lights	Observation at electrodes
P	Yes	grey solid formed at negative electrode
Q	No	no reaction
R	Yes	a gas formed at both electrodes

(*a*) Identify **P**.

____ **1**

(*b*) What type of bonding is present in **Q**?

____ **1**

(*c*) Name the gas formed at the negative electrode when solution **R** is used.

____ **1**

(*d*) What process would be used to obtain a sample of ethanol from the ethanol solution?

____ **1**

(4)

DO NOT WRITE IN THIS MARGIN

Marks | KU | PS

14. Propene has the structural formula shown below.

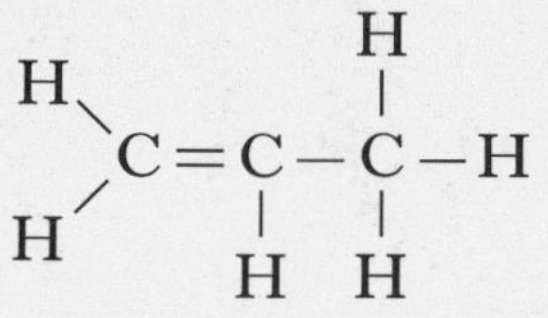

Propene quickly decolourises bromine water, $Br_2(aq)$.

(*a*) (i) Name the type of chemical reaction which takes place when propene reacts with bromine water.

____ **1**

(ii) Draw the **full** structural formula for the product of the reaction.

1

(*b*) Propene can be converted into the polymer, poly(propene).

Complete the diagram to show how **three** propene molecules join to form part of the polymer chain.

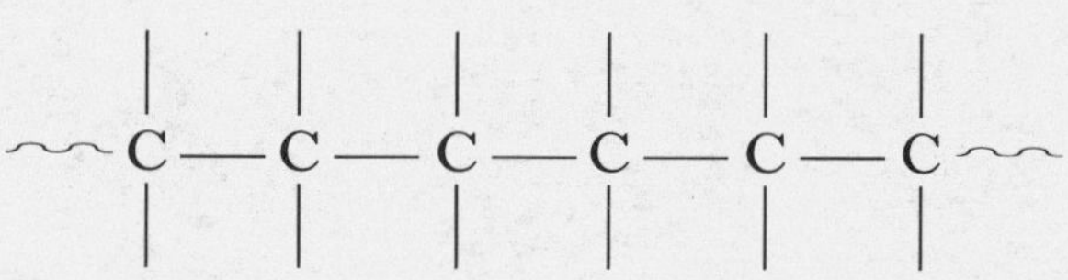

1

(3)

[Turn over

DO NOT WRITE IN THIS MARGIN

Marks KU PS

15. Bones are formed when calcium ions and phosphate ions combine to form insoluble calcium phosphate, $Ca_3(PO_4)_2$.

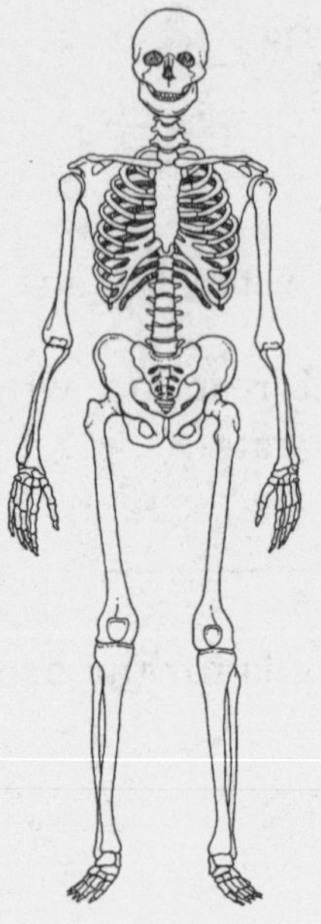

This reaction can be reproduced in the laboratory by adding a solution of calcium chloride to a solution of sodium phosphate.

$$3Ca^{2+}(aq) + 6Cl^{-}(aq) + 6Na^{+}(aq) + 2PO_4^{3-}(aq) \rightarrow 6Na^{+}(aq) + 6Cl^{-}(aq) + (Ca^{2+})_3(PO_4^{3-})_2(s)$$

(*a*) Circle the spectator ions in the above equation. **1**

(*b*) What technique could be used to remove the calcium phosphate from the mixture?

____ **1**

(*c*) Calculate the percentage by mass of calcium in calcium phosphate, $Ca_3(PO_4)_2$.

Answer: ______________ % **2**

(4)

DO NOT WRITE IN THIS MARGIN

Marks KU PS

16. Helen set up the cell shown below.

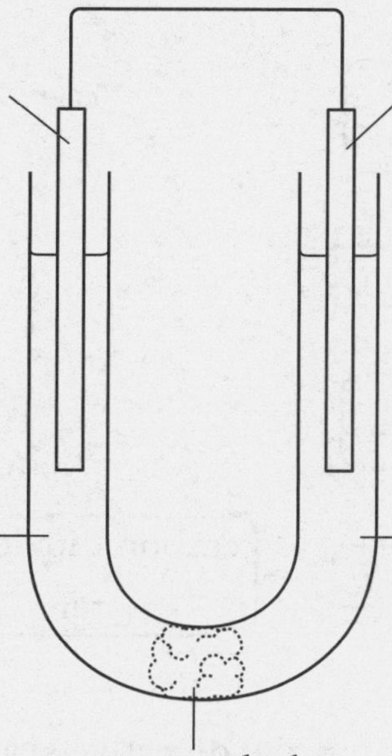

The reaction taking place at electrode **A** is

$$Fe^{3+}(aq) \quad + \quad e^{-} \quad \rightarrow \quad Fe^{2+}(aq)$$

(*a*) (i) **On the diagram**, clearly mark the path and the direction of electron flow. **1**

(ii) What term is used to describe the type of chemical reaction taking place at electrode **A**?

____ **1**

(*b*) Iodine forms at electrode **B**.

(i) What would you **see** happening around electrode **B**?

____

____ **1**

(ii) Write an ion-electron equation for the chemical reaction taking place at electrode **B**.

You may wish to use the data booklet to help you.

____ **1**

(4)

[Turn over

DO NOT WRITE IN THIS MARGIN

Marks KU PS

17. The flow diagram shows what happens to starchy foods after they have been eaten.

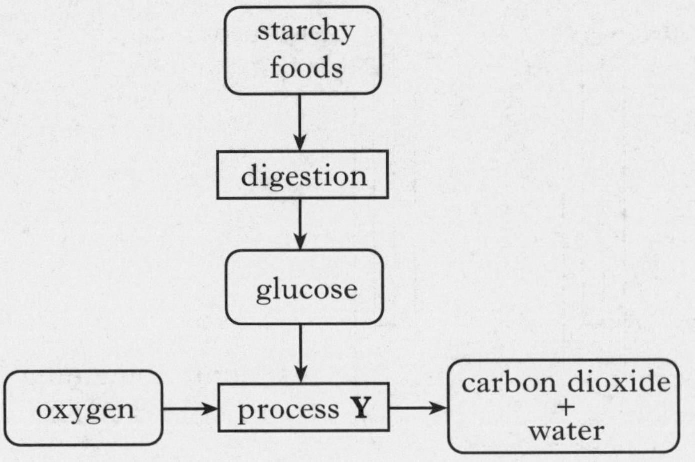

(*a*) What **type** of substance, present in the digestive system, speeds up the breakdown of starchy foods?

____ **1**

(*b*) What **type** of chemical reaction takes place when starch is broken down into glucose during digestion?

____ **1**

(*c*) Process **Y** provides the body with energy.

Name this process.

____ **1**

(*d*) Name an isomer of glucose.

____ **1**

(4)

DO NOT WRITE IN THIS MARGIN

Marks KU PS

18. The energy required to remove an outer electron from an atom is called the ionisation energy.

(*a*) The equation for the ionisation of a magnesium atom is

$$Mg(g) \longrightarrow Mg^{+}(g) + e^{-}$$

Write the electron arrangement for $Mg^{+}(g)$.

______________________________________ **1**

(*b*) The graph shows the ionisation energy values for the first 20 elements.

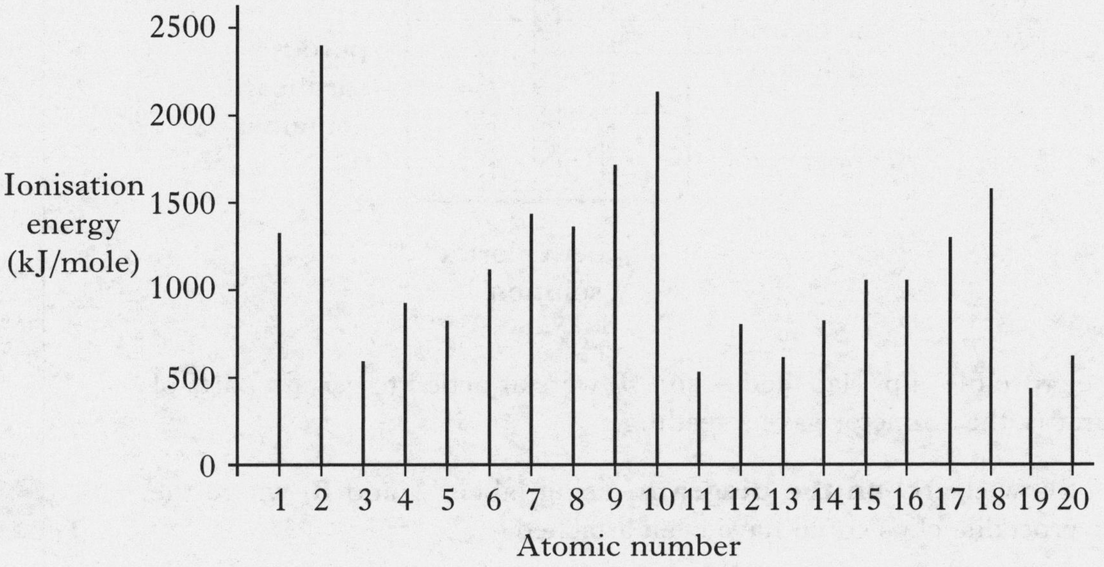

(i) Describe the general trend in ionisation energy going from lithium to neon.

____

____

______________________________________ **1**

(ii) Describe the trend in ionisation energy going down a group.

____

____

______________________________________ **1**

(3)

[Turn over

DO NOT WRITE IN THIS MARGIN

Marks | KU | PS

19. Roy wanted to show that chemicals can be used to produce an electric current.

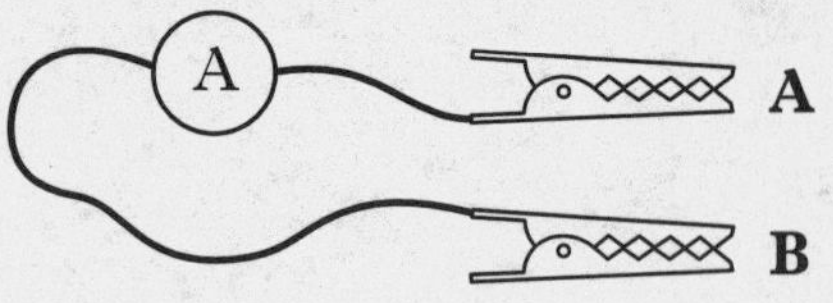

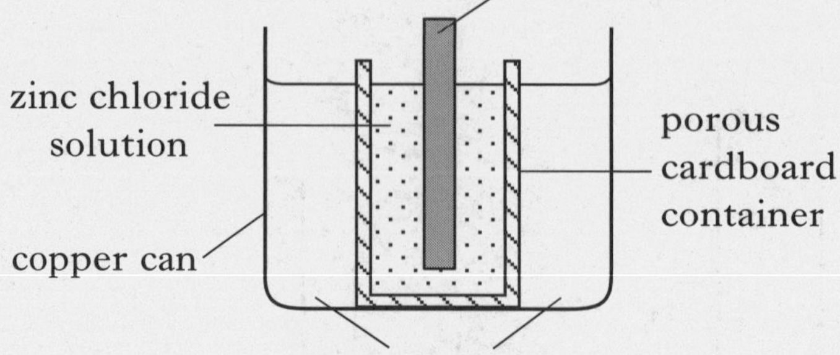

When the crocodile clips (labelled **A** and **B**) were attached to certain parts of the apparatus, the ammeter gave a reading.

(*a*) (i) Show clearly **on the diagram**, using labels **A** and **B**, where the crocodile clips could have been attached. **1**

(ii) Why was no current produced when the porous cardboard container was replaced by a glass beaker?

____

____

____ **1**

(iii) What would happen to the reading on the ammeter if the zinc rod was replaced with a tin rod in a tin chloride solution?

____ **1**

DO NOT WRITE IN THIS MARGIN

Marks | KU | PS

19. (continued)

(*b*) Roy was instructed to make 50 cm^3 of a 1 mol/litre solution of copper chloride, $CuCl_2$.

Calculate the mass, in grams, of copper chloride needed.

Show your working clearly

Answer: ____________ g **2**

(5)

[*END OF QUESTION PAPER*]

DO NOT WRITE IN THIS MARGIN

KU	PS

ADDITIONAL SPACE FOR ANSWERS

ADDITIONAL GRAPH PAPER FOR QUESTION 12(*a*)

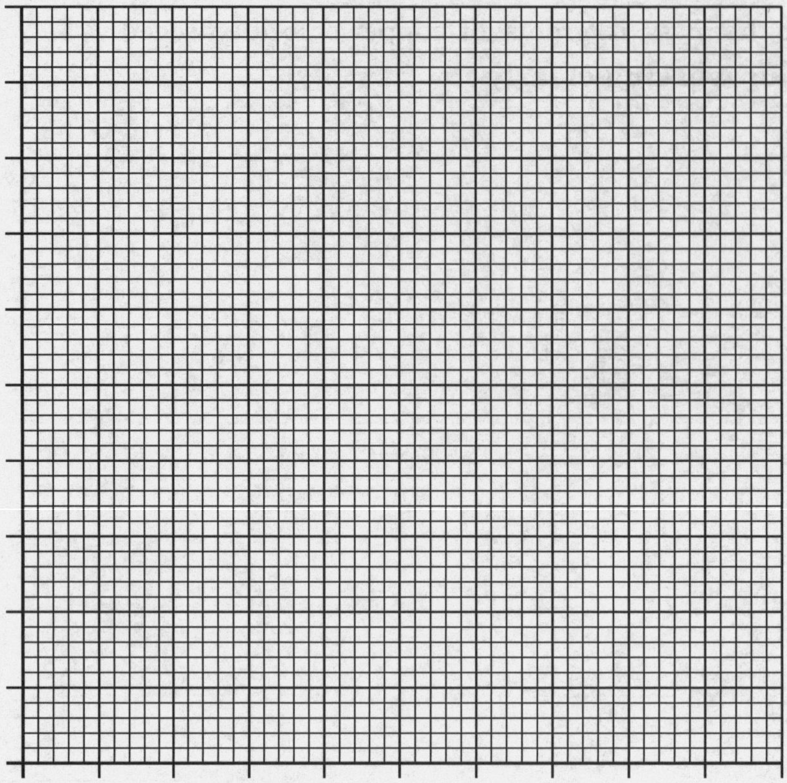

2004 | Credit

[BLANK PAGE]

FOR OFFICIAL USE

C

	KU	PS
Total Marks		

0500/402

NATIONAL QUALIFICATIONS 2004

MONDAY, 10 MAY
10.50 AM – 12.20 PM

CHEMISTRY STANDARD GRADE

Credit Level

Fill in these boxes and read what is printed below.

Full name of centre

Town

Forename(s)

Surname

Date of birth
Day Month Year

Scottish candidate number

Number of seat

1 All questions should be attempted.

2 Necessary data will be found in the Data Booklet provided for Chemistry at Standard Grade and Intermediate 2.

3 The questions may be answered in any order but all answers are to be written in this answer book, and must be written clearly and legibly in ink.

4 Rough work, if any should be necessary, as well as the fair copy, is to be written in this book.
Rough work should be scored through when the fair copy has been written.

5 Additional space for answers and rough work will be found at the end of the book.

6 The size of the space provided for an answer should not be taken as an indication of how much to write. It is not necessary to use all the space.

7 Before leaving the examination room you must give this book to the invigilator. If you do not, you may lose all the marks for this paper.

SCOTTISH QUALIFICATIONS AUTHORITY

SAB 0500/402 6/26270

PART 1

In Questions 1 to 9 of this part of the paper, an answer is given by circling the appropriate letter (or letters) in the answer grid provided.

In some questions, two letters are required for full marks.

If more than the correct number of answers is given, marks will be deducted.

A total of 20 marks is available in this part of the paper.

SAMPLE QUESTION

A CH_4	B H_2	C CO_2
D CO	E C_2H_5OH	F C

(*a*) Identify the hydrocarbon.

(A)	B	C
D	E	F

The correct answer to part (*a*) is A. This should be circled.

(*b*) Identify the **two** elements.

A	(B)	C
D	E	(F)

As indicated in this question, there are **two** correct answers to part (*b*). These are B and F. Both answers are circled.

If, after you have recorded your answer, you decide that you have made an error and wish to make a change, you should cancel the original answer and circle the answer you now consider to be correct. Thus, in part (*a*), if you want to change an answer A to an answer D, your answer sheet would look like this:

~~(A)~~	B	C
(D)	E	F

If you want to change back to an answer which has already been scored out, you should enter a tick (✓) in the box of the answer of your choice, thus:

✓ ~~(A)~~	B	C
~~(D)~~	E	F

DO NOT WRITE IN THIS MARGIN

Marks | KU | PS

1. The grid shows the formulae of six oxides.

A H_2O	B NO_2	C K_2O
D CaO	E CO	F SO_2

(*a*) Identify the oxide produced by the sparking of air in car engines.

A	B	C
D	E	F

1

(*b*) Identify the **two** oxides produced by burning hydrocarbons.

A	B	C
D	E	F

1

(2)

[Turn over

DO NOT WRITE IN THIS MARGIN

Marks KU PS

2. The names of some hydrocarbons are shown in the grid.

A cyclobutane	B cyclopentane	C butane
D propane	E ethane	F butene

(*a*) Identify the hydrocarbon which is a liquid at 25 °C.

You may wish to use the data booklet to help you.

A	B	C
D	E	F

1

(*b*) Identify the **two** isomers.

A	B	C
D	E	F

1

(*c*) Identify the hydrocarbon that reacts quickly with bromine solution.

A	B	C
D	E	F

1

(3)

DO NOT WRITE IN THIS MARGIN

Marks | KU | PS

3. The grid shows the names of some soluble compounds.

A magnesium bromide	B sodium bromide	C lithium hydroxide
D sodium iodide	E potassium sulphate	F lithium chloride

(*a*) Identify the base.

A	B	C
D	E	F

1

(*b*) Identify the **two** compounds whose solutions would form a precipitate when mixed.

You may wish to use the data booklet to help you.

A	B	C
D	E	F

1

(*c*) Identify the compound with a formula of the type $\mathbf{XY_2}$, where **X** is a metal.

A	B	C
D	E	F

1

(3)

[Turn over

DO NOT WRITE IN THIS MARGIN

Marks KU PS

4. A pupil carried out the following experiments.

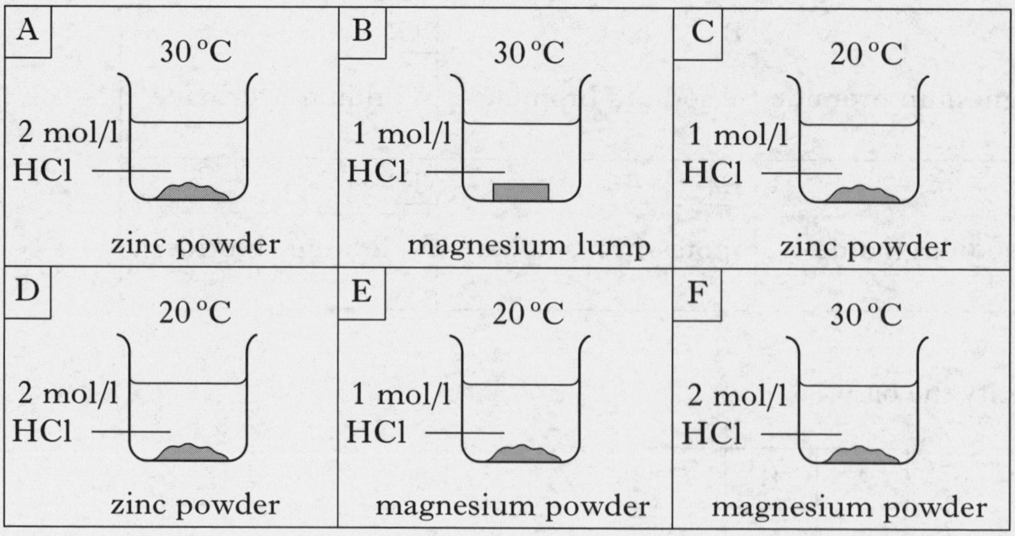

(*a*) Identify the **two** experiments which can be used to investigate the effect of concentration on the rate of the reaction.

A	B	C
D	E	F

1

(*b*) Identify the experiment with the fastest reaction rate.

A	B	C
D	E	F

1
(2)

DO NOT WRITE IN THIS MARGIN

Marks KU PS

5. The table contains information about some substances.

Substance	Melting point/°C	Boiling point/°C	Conducts as a solid	Conducts as a liquid
A	455	1567	no	yes
B	80	218	no	no
C	1492	2897	yes	yes
D	1407	2357	no	no
E	645	1287	no	yes
F	98	890	yes	yes

(*a*) Identify the **two** ionic compounds.

A
B
C
D
E
F

1

(*b*) Identify the substance which exists as a covalent network.

A
B
C
D
E
F

1

(2)

[Turn over

DO NOT WRITE IN THIS MARGIN

Marks | KU | PS

6. The grid shows information about some particles.

A $^{34}_{16}S^{2-}$	B $^{24}_{12}Mg^{2+}$	C $^{39}_{19}K$
D $^{40}_{19}K$	E $^{40}_{20}Ca$	F $^{35}_{17}Cl^{-}$

(*a*) Identify the **two** particles which are isotopes.

A	B	C
D	E	F

1

(*b*) Identify the **two** particles with the same electron arrangement as argon.

A	B	C
D	E	F

1

(2)

DO NOT WRITE IN THIS MARGIN

Marks | KU | PS

7. The grid contains information about the particles found in atoms.

A charge = zero	B relative mass almost zero	C charge = 1–
D found inside the nucleus	E charge = 1+	F relative mass = 1

Identify the **two** terms which can be applied to electrons.

A	B	C
D	E	F

(2)

[Turn over

DO NOT WRITE IN THIS MARGIN

Marks KU PS

8. Glucose, sucrose and starch are carbohydrates.

Identify the **two** correct statements.

A	Glucose molecules join together with the loss of water.
B	Starch is a polymer made from sucrose molecules.
C	Sucrose turns warm Benedict's solution orange.
D	Glucose is an isomer of sucrose.
E	Starch dissolves easily in water.
F	Sucrose can be hydrolysed.

A
B
C
D
E
F

(2)

DO NOT WRITE IN THIS MARGIN

Marks KU PS

9. The diagram shows how an object can be coated in nickel.

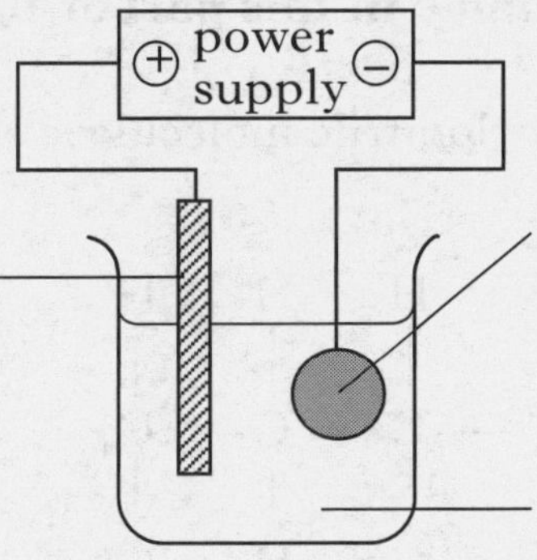

The following reactions take place at the electrodes.

Negative electrode: $Ni^{2+}(aq) + 2e^{-} \rightarrow Ni(s)$

Positive electrode: $Ni(s) \rightarrow Ni^{2+}(aq) + 2e^{-}$

Identify the **two** correct statements.

A	Nickel ions move towards the nickel electrode.
B	The mass of the nickel electrode decreases.
C	The process is an example of galvanising.
D	Oxidation occurs at the nickel electrode.
E	Electrons flow through the solution.

A
B
C
D
E

(2)

[Turn over

DO NOT WRITE IN THIS MARGIN

Marks | KU | PS

PART 2

A total of 40 marks is available in this part of the paper.

10. The structure of part of a polyacrylonitrile molecule is shown below.

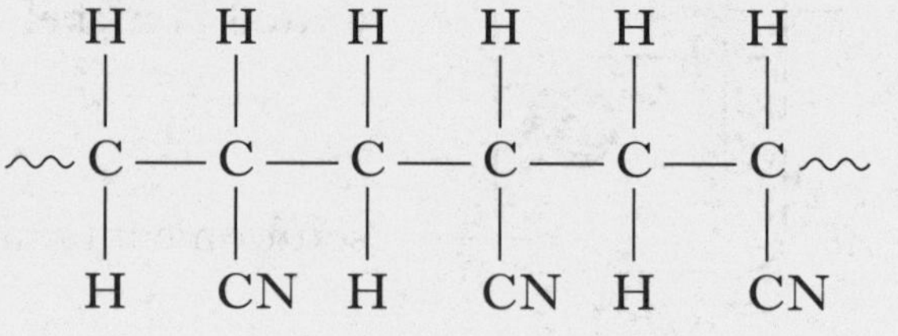

(*a*) Draw the structural formula for the monomer used to make polyacrylonitrile. **1**

(*b*) Name a toxic gas produced when polyacrylonitrile burns.

____ **1**

(2)

DO NOT WRITE IN THIS MARGIN

Marks KU PS

11. Some Euro coins are made from a hard-wearing alloy called Nordic Gold.

(*a*) What is an alloy?

____

____ **1**

(*b*) The composition of Nordic Gold is shown in the table.

Metal	copper	aluminium	zinc	tin
% by mass	89	5	5	1

One of the coins has a mass of 5·74 g.

(i) Calculate the mass, in grams, of aluminium in the coin.
Show your working clearly.

__________ g **1**

(ii) Calculate the number of moles of aluminium in the coin.
Show your working clearly.

__________ mol **1**

(3)

[Turn over

Marks KU PS

12. A group of pupils investigated the speed of reaction between marble chips (calcium carbonate) and hydrochloric acid, concentration 1 mol/l.

They used excess hydrochloric acid to make sure all the calcium carbonate had been used up.

The pupils used a balance to measure the mass lost during the reaction.

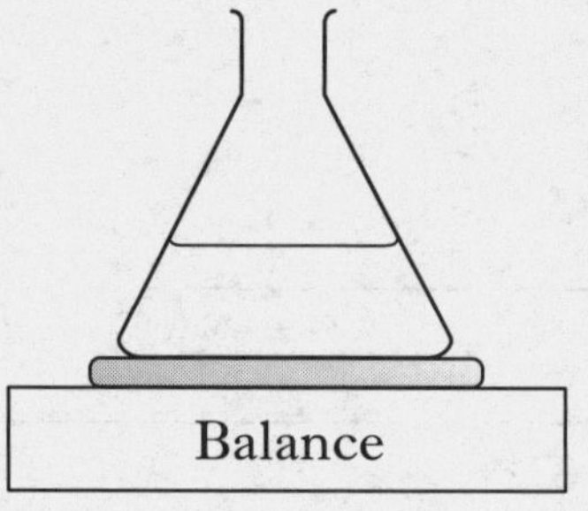

The results are shown in the table.

Time/minutes	0	0·5	1·0	2·0	3·0	4·0	5·0
Mass lost/g	0	0·30	0·50	0·70	0·76	0·79	0·80

(*a*) Why is mass lost during the reaction?

____

____ **1**

DO NOT WRITE IN THIS MARGIN

Marks KU PS

12. (continued)

(*b*) Draw a line graph of the results.

Use appropriate scales to fill most of the graph paper.

(Additional graph paper, if required, will be found on page 26.)

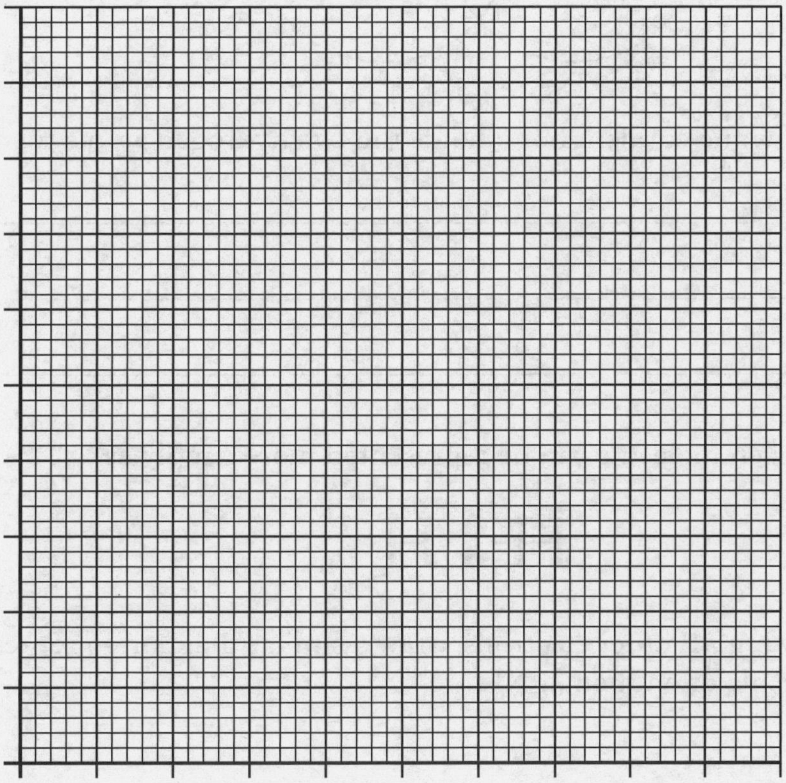

2

(*c*) The experiment was repeated using the same volume of hydrochloric acid, but with a concentration of 2 mol/l.

What mass loss would have been recorded?

________ g **1**

(*d*) Name the salt produced when marble chips react with hydrochloric acid.

______________________________________ **1**

(5)

[Turn over

DO NOT WRITE IN THIS MARGIN

Marks	KU	PS

13. In a hydrogen molecule the atoms share two electrons in a covalent bond.

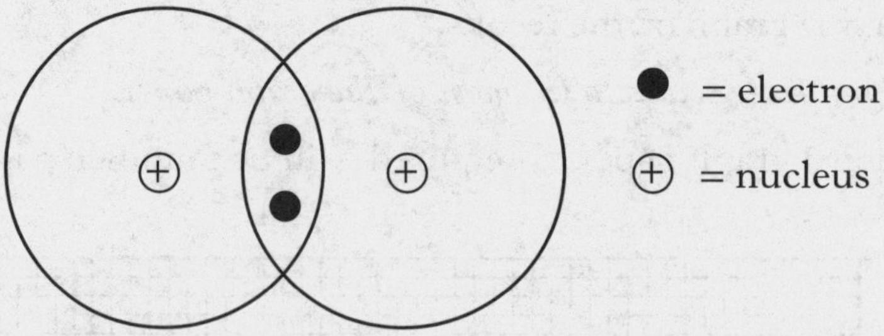

(*a*) Explain how the covalent bond holds the two hydrogen atoms together.

____

____

____ **1**

(*b*) The hydrogen molecule can be represented more simply as

(i) Showing **all** outer electrons, draw a similar diagram to represent a molecule of ammonia, NH_3.

1

(ii) Draw another diagram to show the **shape** of an ammonia molecule.

1

(3)

DO NOT WRITE IN THIS MARGIN

Marks | KU | PS

14. Methanol can take part in many chemical reactions.

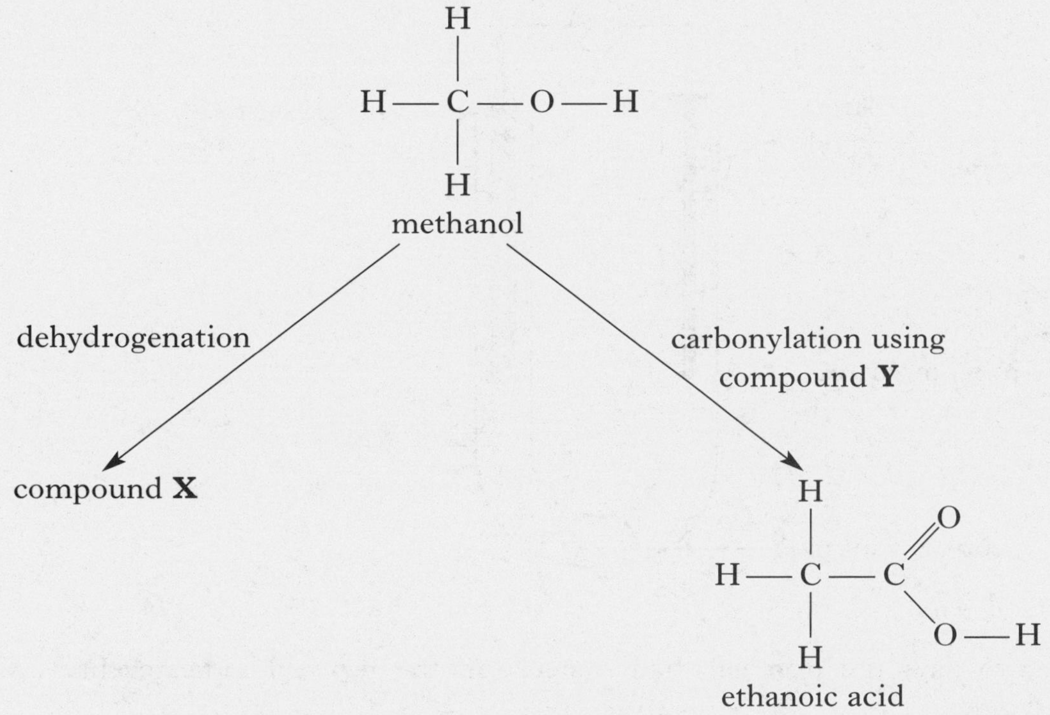

(*a*) (i) Compound **X** has the molecular formula CH_2O.
Draw the full structural formula for compound **X**. **1**

(ii) Methanol is changed to compound **X** by dehydrogenation.
Suggest what is meant by **dehydrogenation**.

____

____

______________________________________ **1**

(*b*) In carbonylation, methanol reacts with compound **Y** forming only ethanoic acid.
Suggest a name for compound **Y**.

______________________________________ **1**

(3)

DO NOT WRITE IN THIS MARGIN

Marks KU PS

15. Gemma and Laura set up the simple cell shown below.

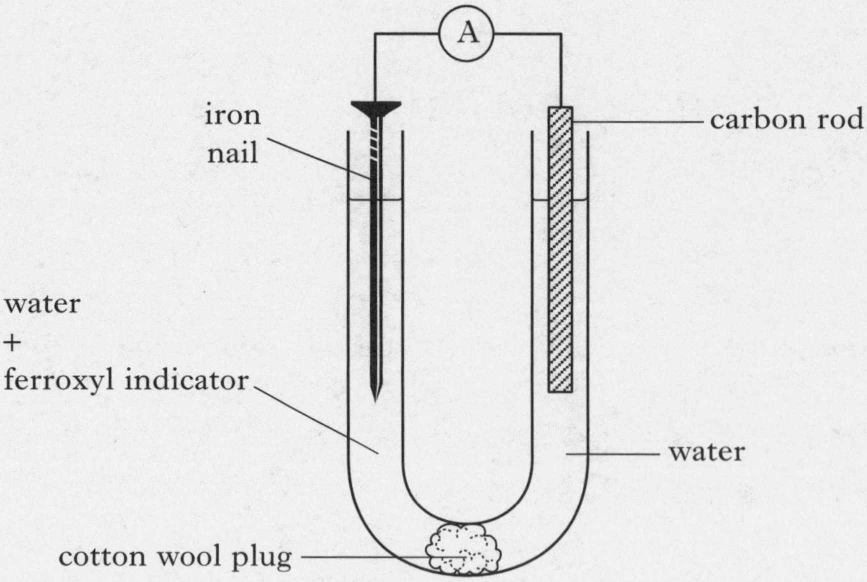

After two days the iron nail had rusted and the ferroxyl indicator had turned blue.

(*a*) **On the diagram**, clearly mark the path and direction of electron flow. **1**

(*b*) The reaction taking place at the carbon rod produces hydroxide ions.

How could Gemma and Laura have shown that hydroxide ions were present?

____

____ **1**

(2)

DO NOT WRITE IN THIS MARGIN

Marks KU PS

16. Electrolysis is a common industrial process. Some uses of electrolysis are shown in the diagram.

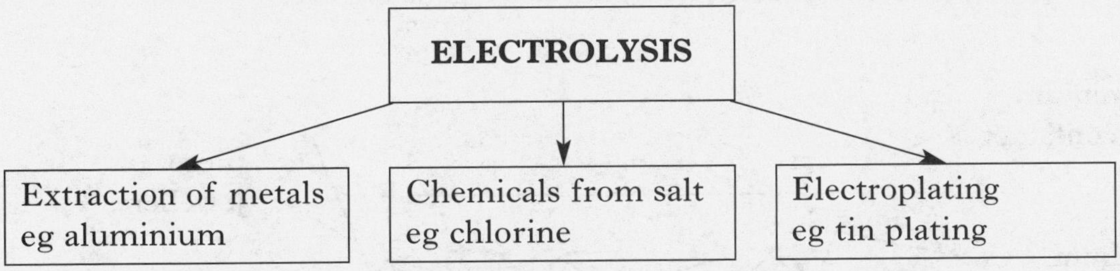

(*a*) State what is meant by electrolysis. **1**

(*b*) Aluminium is extracted by electrolysis of its molten oxide since aluminium oxide does not react when heated with carbon.

Why does aluminium oxide **not** react with hot carbon? **1**

(*c*) Chlorine is produced by the electrolysis of sodium chloride solution.

Write the ion-electron equation for the formation of chlorine.

You may wish to use the data booklet to help you. **1**

(*d*) Tin plated iron rusts very rapidly if the plating is scratched.

Explain why the iron rusts so rapidly. **2**

(5)

[Turn over

DO NOT WRITE IN THIS MARGIN

Marks | KU | PS

17. Silver jewellery slowly tarnishes in air. This is due to the formation of silver(I) sulphide, Ag_2S.

The silver(I) sulphide can be converted back to silver as follows.

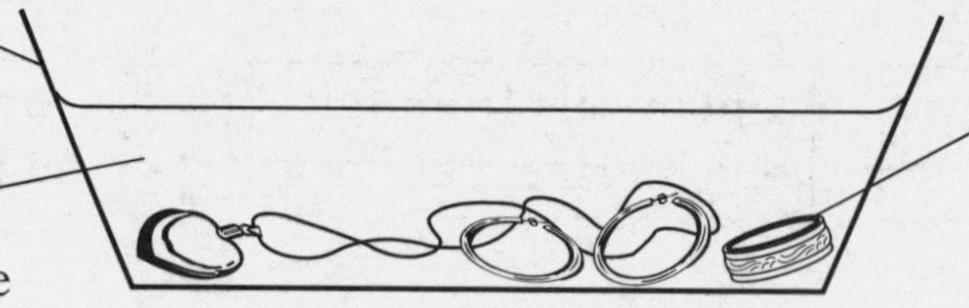

(*a*) Write the ionic formula for sodium hydrogencarbonate.
You may wish to use the data booklet to help you.

______________________________ 1

(*b*) The equation for the reaction which takes place in the aluminium container is:

$$Ag_2S \quad + \quad Al \quad \rightarrow \quad Ag \quad + \quad Al_2S_3$$

(i) Balance this equation. 1

(ii) Name the type of chemical reaction which takes place.

______________________________ 1

(*c*) Calculate the percentage by mass of aluminium in Al_2S_3.
Show your working clearly.

2

(5)

DO NOT WRITE IN THIS MARGIN

Marks | KU | PS

18. Fritz was investigating the properties of ammonia.

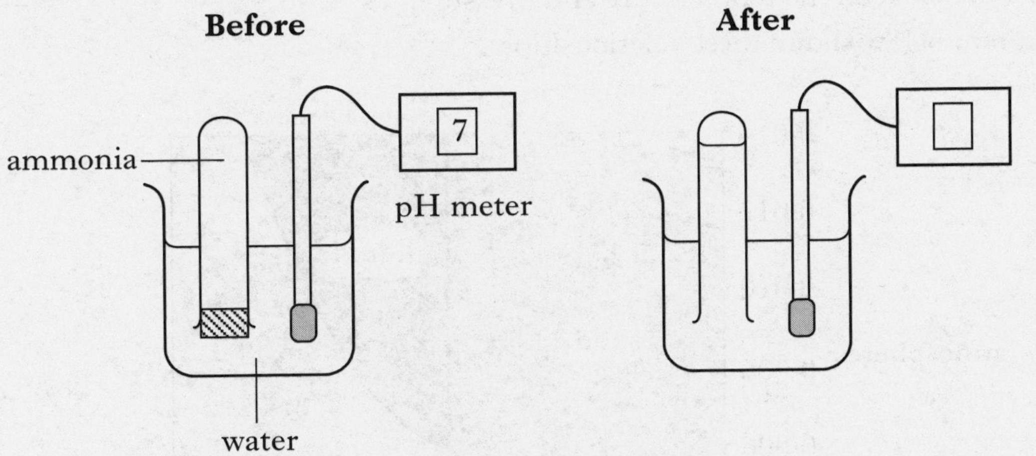

(*a*) Why did the water rise up the test tube when the stopper was removed?

____

____ **1**

(*b*) When the stopper was removed the reading on the pH meter changed. Suggest what the new reading would have been.

__________________________ **1**

(2)

[Turn over

DO NOT WRITE IN THIS MARGIN

Marks | KU | PS

19. Water can exist in three different states: solid, liquid and gas.

The state depends on the temperature and pressure.

The diagram below shows these relationships.

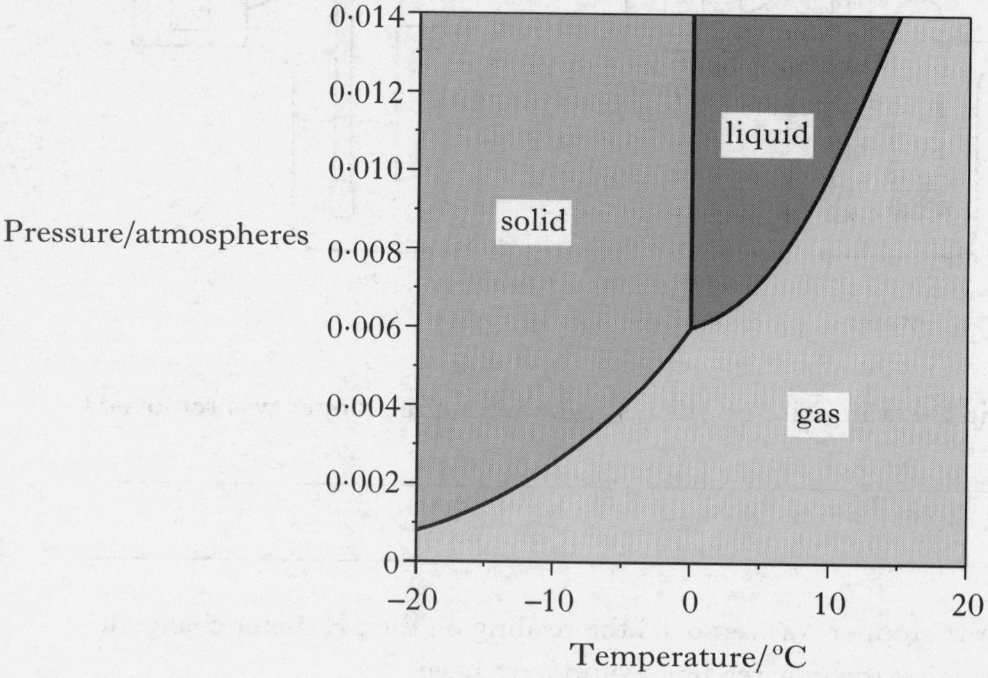

(*a*) In which state would water exist at 15 °C and 0·007 atmospheres?

____________________________________ **1**

(*b*) Solid water at 0·004 atmospheres is allowed to warm up. The pressure is kept constant.

At what temperature would the solid water change into a gas?

__________ °C **1**

(2)

DO NOT WRITE IN THIS MARGIN

Marks KU PS

20. Dienes are a homologous series of hydrocarbons which contain two double bonds per molecule.

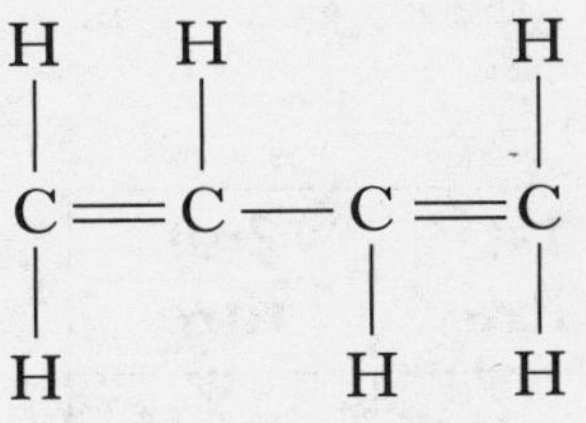

buta-1,3-diene

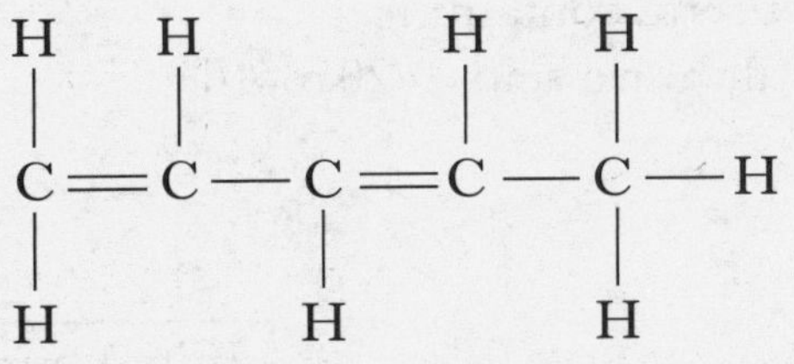

penta-1,3-diene

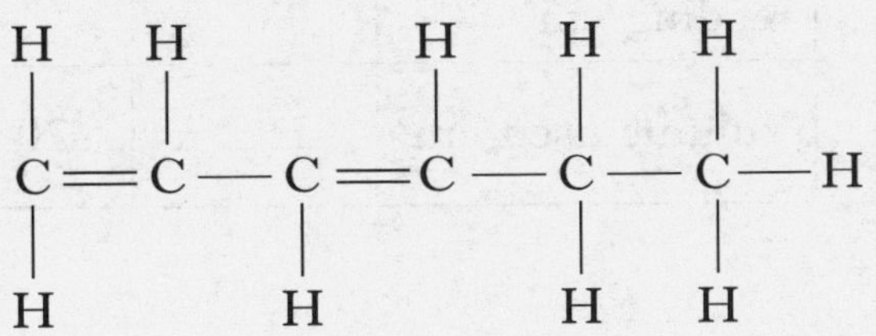

hexa-1,3-diene

(*a*) What is meant by the term "homologous series"?

____

____

____ **1**

(*b*) Suggest a general formula for the dienes.

________________________ **1**

(*c*) Write the **molecular formula** for the product of the complete reaction of penta-1,3-diene with bromine.

________________________ **1**

(*d*) Draw a full structural formula for an isomer of buta-1,3-diene which contains only **one** double bond per molecule.

1

(4)

DO NOT WRITE IN THIS MARGIN

Marks | KU | PS

21. A pupil carried out a titration using the chemicals and apparatus shown below.

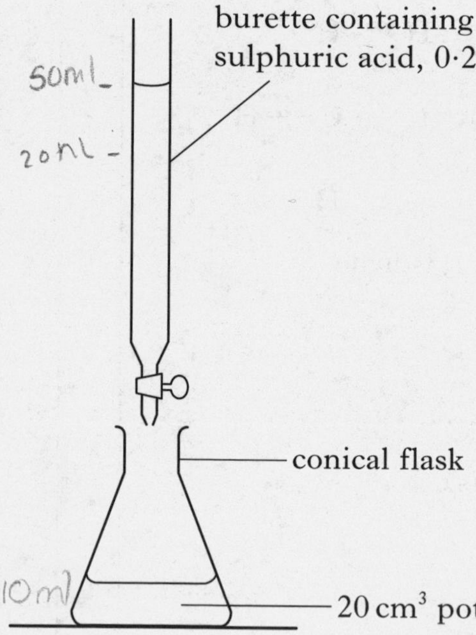

	Rough titre	**1st titre**	**2nd titre**
Initial burette reading/cm³	0·5	21·7	0·3
Final burette reading/cm³	21·7	42·4	20·8
Volume used/cm³	21·2	20·7	20·5

(*a*) How would the pupil know when to stop adding acid from the burette?

____

____ **1**

(*b*) (i) What average volume should be used to calculate the number of moles of sulphuric acid needed to neutralise the potassium hydroxide solution?

__________ cm³ **1**

DO NOT WRITE IN THIS MARGIN

Marks KU PS

21. (*b*) (continued)

(ii) Calculate the number of moles of sulphuric acid in this average volume.

Show your working clearly.

_________ mol **1**

(iii) The equation for the titration reaction is

$$H_2SO_4 \quad + \quad 2KOH \quad \rightarrow \quad K_2SO_4 \quad + \quad 2H_2O$$

Calculate the number of moles of potassium hydroxide in $20\,cm^3$ of the potassium hydroxide solution.

Show your working clearly.

_________ mol **1**

(4)

[*END OF QUESTION PAPER*]

DO NOT WRITE IN THIS MARGIN

KU	PS

ADDITIONAL SPACE FOR ANSWERS

ADDITIONAL GRAPH PAPER FOR QUESTION 12(*b*)

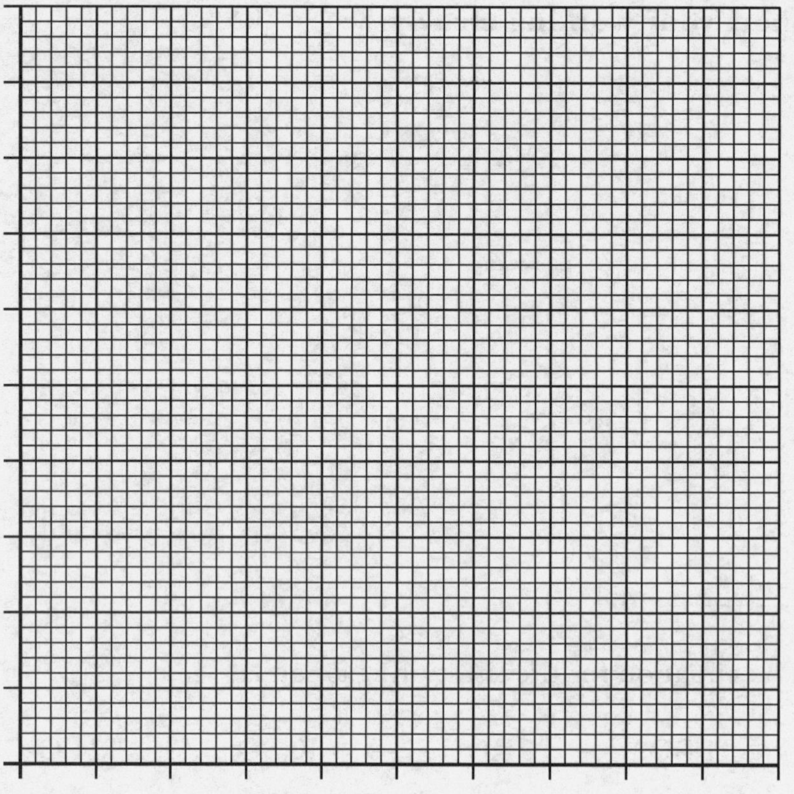

BLANK PAGE

FOR OFFICIAL USE

C

	KU	PS
Total Marks		

0500/402

NATIONAL QUALIFICATIONS 2005

MONDAY, 9 MAY
10.50 AM – 12.20 PM

CHEMISTRY
STANDARD GRADE
Credit Level

Fill in these boxes and read what is printed below.

Full name of centre

Town

Forename(s)

Surname

Date of birth
Day Month Year

Scottish candidate number

Number of seat

1 All questions should be attempted.

2 Necessary data will be found in the Data Booklet provided for Chemistry at Standard Grade and Intermediate 2.

3 The questions may be answered in any order but all answers are to be written in this answer book, and must be written clearly and legibly in ink.

4 Rough work, if any should be necessary, as well as the fair copy, is to be written in this book.

Rough work should be scored through when the fair copy has been written.

5 Additional space for answers and rough work will be found at the end of the book.

6 The size of the space provided for an answer should not be taken as an indication of how much to write. It is not necessary to use all the space.

7 Before leaving the examination room you must give this book to the invigilator. If you do not, you may lose all the marks for this paper.

SCOTTISH QUALIFICATIONS AUTHORITY

SAB 0500/402 6/28670

PART 1

In Questions 1 to 9 of this part of the paper, an answer is given by circling the appropriate letter (or letters) in the answer grid provided.

In some questions, two letters are required for full marks.

If more than the correct number of answers is given, marks will be deducted.

A total of 20 marks is available in this part of the paper.

SAMPLE QUESTION

A CH_4	B H_2	C CO_2
D CO	E C_2H_5OH	F C

(*a*) Identify the hydrocarbon.

(A)	B	C
D	E	F

The one correct answer to part (*a*) is A. This should be circled.

(*b*) Identify the **two** elements.

A	(B)	C
D	E	(F)

As indicated in this question, there are **two** correct answers to part (*b*). These are B and F. Both answers are circled.

If, after you have recorded your answer, you decide that you have made an error and wish to make a change, you should cancel the original answer and circle the answer you now consider to be correct. Thus, in part (*a*), if you want to change an answer A to an answer D, your answer sheet would look like this:

~~(A)~~	B	C
(D)	E	F

If you want to change back to an answer which has already been scored out, you should enter a tick (✓) in the box of the answer of your choice, thus:

✓ ~~(A)~~	B	C
~~(D)~~	E	F

DO NOT WRITE IN THIS MARGIN

Marks KU PS

1. The grid shows the names of some elements.

A argon	B potassium	C magnesium
D chlorine	E phosphorus	F sulphur

(*a*) Identify the element which produces a lilac flame colour.
You may wish to use the data booklet to help you.

A	B	C
D	E	F

1

(*b*) Identify the element with atoms which have the same electron arrangement as a Ca^{2+} ion.

A	B	C
D	E	F

1

(*c*) Identify the **two** elements which would form a covalent compound with a formula of the type $\mathbf{X_3Y_2}$.

A	B	C
D	E	F

1

(3)

[Turn over

DO NOT WRITE IN THIS MARGIN

Marks | KU | PS

2. Distillation of crude oil produces several fractions.

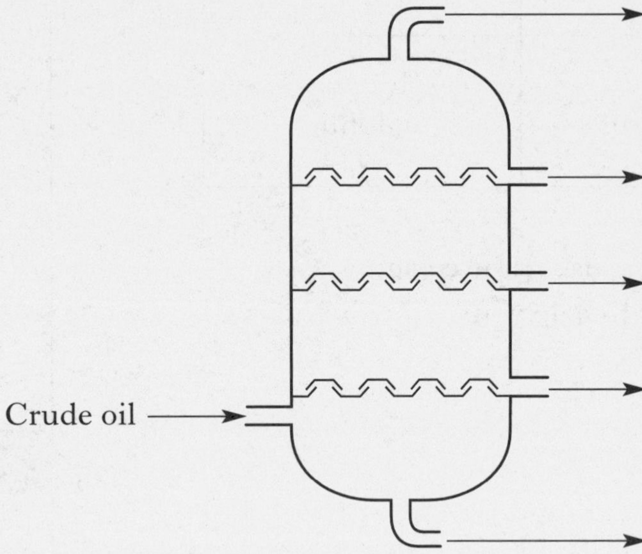

Fraction	Number of carbon atoms per molecule
A	1–4
B	4–10
C	10–16
D	16–20
E	20+

(*a*) Identify the fraction which is used as a fuel in camping gas stoves.

A
B
C
D
E

1

(*b*) Identify the fraction with the highest viscosity.

A
B
C
D
E

1

(2)

DO NOT WRITE IN THIS MARGIN

Marks KU PS

3. The names of some carbohydrates are shown.

A	glucose
B	fructose
C	maltose
D	sucrose
E	starch

(*a*) Identify the carbohydrate which does not dissolve well in water.

A
B
C
D
E

1

(*b*) Identify the **two** carbohydrates which are disaccharides.

A
B
C
D
E

1

(2)

[Turn over

DO NOT WRITE IN THIS MARGIN

Marks | KU | PS

4. The table contains information about some substances.

Substance	Melting point/°C	Boiling point/°C	Conducts as a solid	Conducts as a liquid
A	−7	59	no	no
B	98	883	yes	yes
C	−39	357	yes	yes
D	547	1265	no	yes
E	−78	−33	no	no
F	1700	2230	no	no

(*a*) Identify the substance which is a gas at 0 °C.

A
B
C
D
E
F

1

(*b*) Identify the **two** substances which exist as molecules.

A
B
C
D
E
F

1

(2)

Marks KU PS

5. The grid shows the formulae of some hydrocarbons.

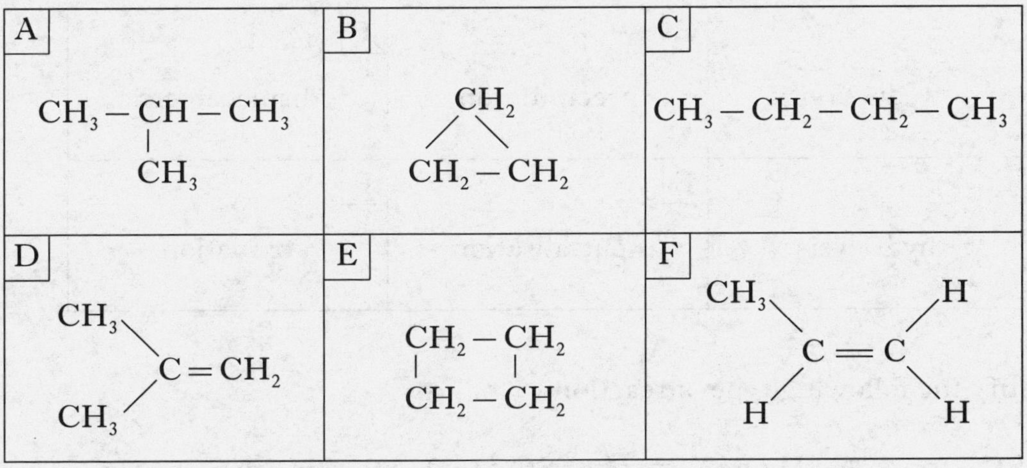

(*a*) Identify the hydrocarbon which can be used to make poly(propene).

A	B	C
D	E	F

1

(*b*) Identify the **two** hydrocarbons with the general formula C_nH_{2n} which do **not** react quickly with bromine solution.

A	B	C
D	E	F

1

(*c*) Identify the **two** isomers of

$$CH_2=CH-CH_2-CH_3$$

A	B	C
D	E	F

2

(4)

[Turn over

DO NOT WRITE IN THIS MARGIN

Marks KU PS

6. There are many different types of chemical reaction.

A reduction	B precipitation	C displacement
D hydrolysis	E neutralisation	F oxidation

Identify the following type of reaction.

$$SO_3^{2-}(aq) + H_2O(\ell) \longrightarrow SO_4^{2-}(aq) + 2H^+(aq) + 2e^-$$

A	B	C
D	E	F

(1)

DO NOT WRITE IN THIS MARGIN

Marks KU PS

7. The grid shows some statements which could be applied to a solution.

A	It does not react with magnesium.
B	It has a pH less than 7.
C	It does not conduct electricity.
D	It produces chlorine gas when electrolysed.
E	It contains more H^+ ions than pure water.

Identify the **two** statements which are true for **both** dilute hydrochloric acid and dilute sulphuric acid.

A
B
C
D
E

(2)

[Turn over

DO NOT WRITE IN THIS MARGIN

Marks KU PS

8. David was studying the reactions of some metals and their compounds.

He carried out experiments involving magnesium, copper, zinc, nickel, silver and an unknown metal **X**.

Listed below are some of the observations he recorded.

A	**X** was more readily oxidised than copper.
B	**X** oxide was more stable to heat than silver oxide.
C	Magnesium displaced **X** from a solution of **X** nitrate.
D	**X** reacted more vigorously than nickel with dilute acid.
E	Compounds of **X** were more readily reduced than compounds of zinc.

From his observations, David produced the following order of reactivity.

magnesium, zinc, nickel, copper, **X**, silver

→ **decreasing activity**

Identify the **two** observations which can be used to show that **X** has been wrongly placed.

A
B
C
D
E

(2)

DO NOT WRITE IN THIS MARGIN

Marks | KU | PS

9. Equations are used to represent chemical reactions.

A	$H^+(aq) + OH^-(aq) \rightarrow H_2O(\ell)$
B	$Fe^{3+}(aq) + e^- \rightarrow Fe^{2+}(aq)$
C	$Fe(s) \rightarrow Fe^{2+}(aq) + 2e^-$
D	$Fe^{2+}(aq) + 2e^- \rightarrow Fe(s)$
E	$H_2(g) \rightarrow 2H^+(aq) + 2e^-$
F	$2H_2O(\ell) + O_2(g) + 4e^- \rightarrow 4OH^-(aq)$

Identify the **two** equations which are involved in the corrosion of iron.

A
B
C
D
E
F

(2)

[Turn over

[Turn over for Question 10 on *Page thirteen*

DO NOT WRITE IN THIS MARGIN

Marks KU PS

PART 2

A total of 40 marks is available in this part of the paper.

10. On some boats the steel propellers have zinc blocks attached to help prevent rusting. The zinc is oxidised, protecting the steel.

(*a*) (i) Write the ion-electron equation for the oxidation of zinc.

You may wish to use the data booklet to help you.

____ **1**

(ii) What name is given to the **type** of protection provided by the zinc?

____ **1**

(*b*) If cobalt is used instead of zinc the steel propeller rusts quickly.

What does this suggest about the reactivity of cobalt compared to iron?

____

____ **1**

(3)

[Turn over

DO NOT WRITE IN THIS MARGIN

Marks | KU | PS

11. Polystyrene is an addition polymer. It is made from the monomer styrene.

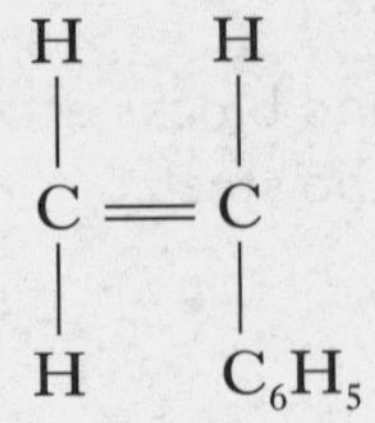

styrene

(*a*) Draw a section of the polystyrene structure, showing three monomer units joined together.

1

(*b*) Calculate the percentage by mass of carbon in a molecule of styrene.

Answer ________________ % **2**

(3)

DO NOT WRITE IN THIS MARGIN

Marks | KU | PS

12. Methane (CH_4), ethane (C_2H_6) and propane (C_3H_8) are the first three members of the alkanes.

(*a*) State the general formula for the alkanes.

______________________________ **1**

(*b*) The ninth member of the alkanes is nonane (C_9H_{20}).

(i) Predict the boiling point of nonane.

You may wish to use page 6 of the data booklet to help you.

__________ °C **1**

(ii) Nonane can be cracked to produce smaller, more useful hydrocarbons. A catalyst is used to speed up this reaction.

Suggest another reason for using a catalyst.

____

______________________________ **1**

(*c*) Alkanes can be made by the reaction of sodium with iodoalkanes.

For example, butane can be made from iodoethane.

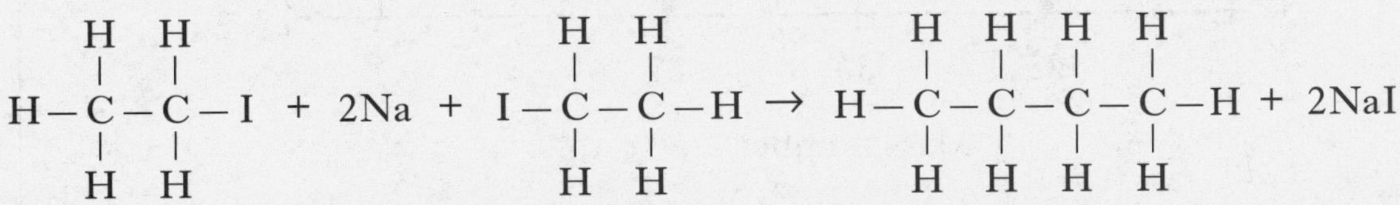

iodoethane + 2Na + iodoethane → butane + 2NaI

Butane can also be made using two **different** iodoalkanes.

Name the **two** iodoalkanes.

____

______________________________ **1**

(4)

[Turn over

DO NOT WRITE IN THIS MARGIN

KU	PS

13. A mass spectrometer is an instrument that can be used to measure the percentage of isotopes in a sample of an element.

When a sample of chlorine is passed through a mass spectrometer the following graph is obtained.

Each spike on the graph shows the presence of an isotope.

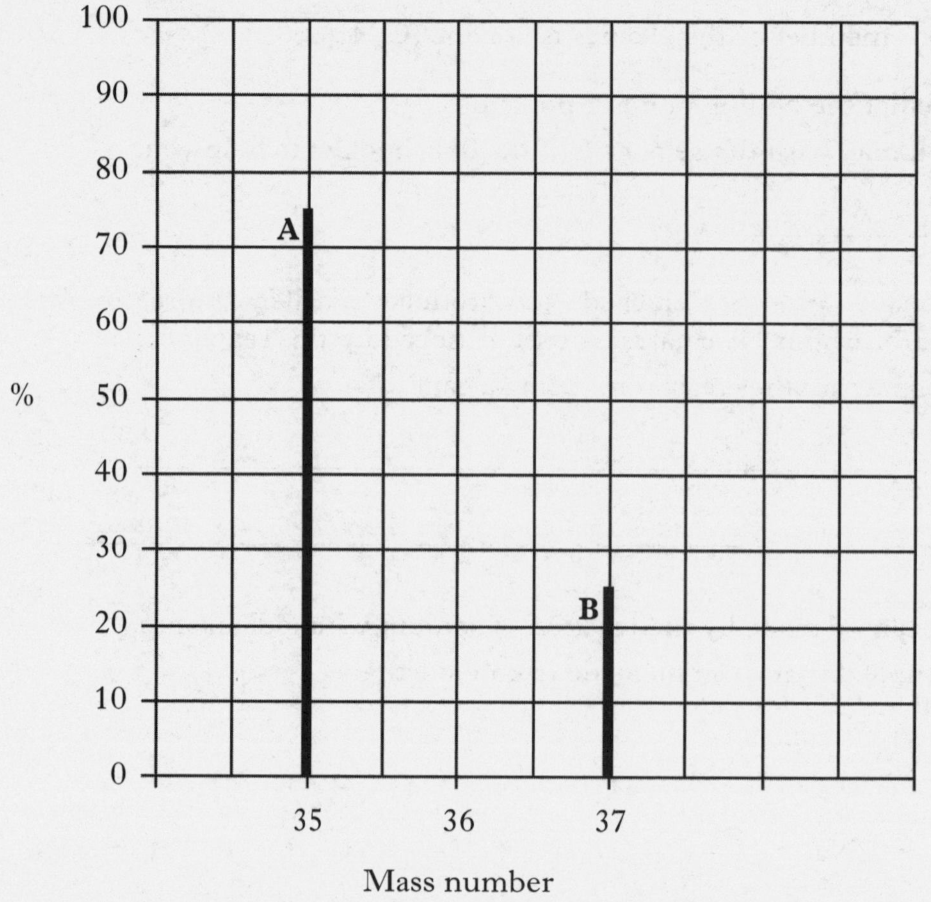

The **relative atomic mass** of an element can be calculated using the formula:

$$\frac{(\text{mass of isotope } \mathbf{A} \times \%) + (\text{mass of isotope } \mathbf{B} \times \%)}{100}$$

The **relative atomic mass** of chlorine $= \frac{(35 \times 75) + (37 \times 25)}{100}$

$= 35{\cdot}5$

DO NOT WRITE IN THIS MARGIN

13. (continued) *Marks* KU PS

(*a*) The following graph was obtained for a sample of lithium.

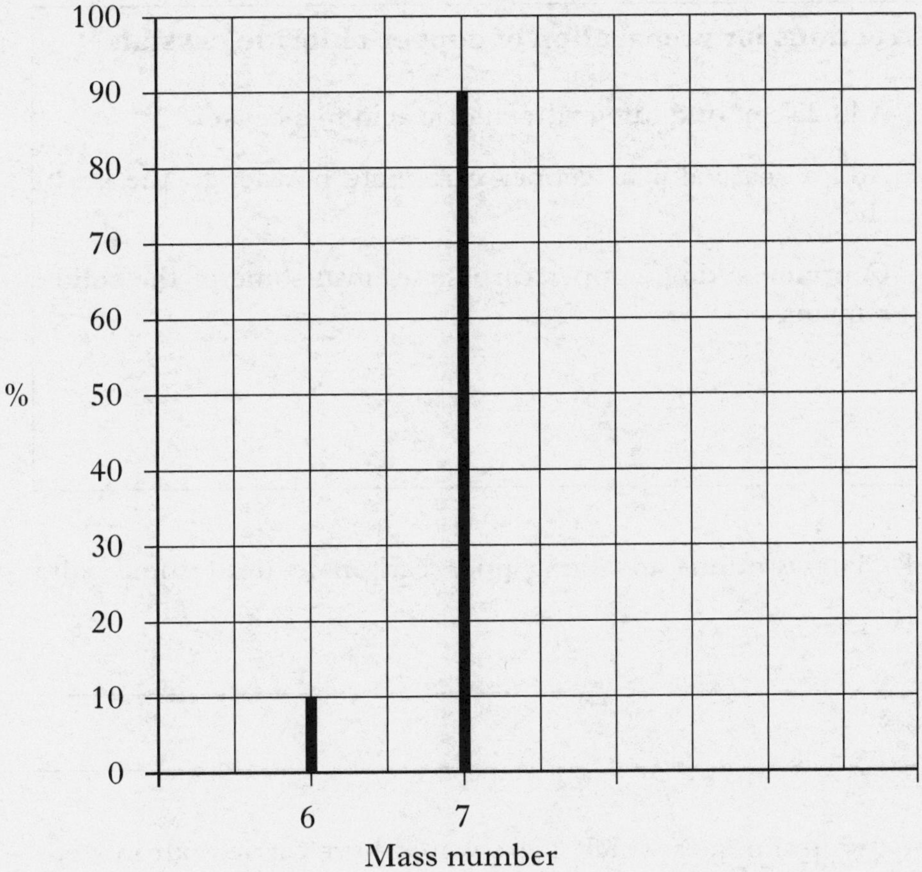

(i) How many isotopes are present in the sample of lithium?

____ 1

(ii) Using the information in the graph calculate the relative atomic mass of lithium.

Show your working clearly. 1

(*b*) Complete the table to show the number of each type of particle in the ion, $^{7}_{3}Li^{+}$.

Particle	**Number**
proton	
neutron	
electron	

2

(4)

DO NOT WRITE IN THIS MARGIN

Marks KU PS

14. Clare carried out an experiment to make copper chloride crystals.

Instructions for preparation of copper chloride crystals	
Step 1	Add 25 cm^3 of dilute hydrochloric acid to a beaker.
Step 2	Add a spatulaful of copper carbonate powder to the acid and stir.
Step 3	Continue adding copper carbonate until some of the solid remains.
Step 4	
Step 5	

(*a*) Why did Clare continue to add copper carbonate until some solid remained?

____

____ **1**

(*b*) Name the **two** techniques which Clare would have carried out in steps **4** and **5** to prepare a sample of copper chloride crystals.

Step 4 ____________________________________

Step 5 ____________________________________ **2**

(3)

DO NOT WRITE IN THIS MARGIN

Marks KU PS

15. Two atoms of nitrogen share electrons to form a nitrogen molecule.

(*a*) Draw a diagram to show how the outer electrons are arranged in a molecule of nitrogen, N_2. **1**

(*b*) Oxides of nitrogen dissolve in water to produce nitric acid.

(i) Name the industrial process used to manufacture nitric acid.

____ **1**

(ii) A platinum catalyst is used in the industrial manufacture of nitric acid.

Why is it **not** necessary to continue heating the platinum once the reaction has started?

____

____ **1**

(3)

[Turn over

DO NOT WRITE IN THIS MARGIN

Marks | KU | PS

16. Dilute hydrochloric acid reacts with sodium thiosulphate solution ($Na_2S_2O_3$) to produce a precipitate of sulphur.

$$HCl + Na_2S_2O_3 \rightarrow NaCl + S + SO_2 + H_2O$$

(*a*) Balance this equation. **1**

(*b*) A pupil investigated the effect of temperature on the speed of the reaction. She measured the time taken for enough sulphur to form to make the cross disappear.

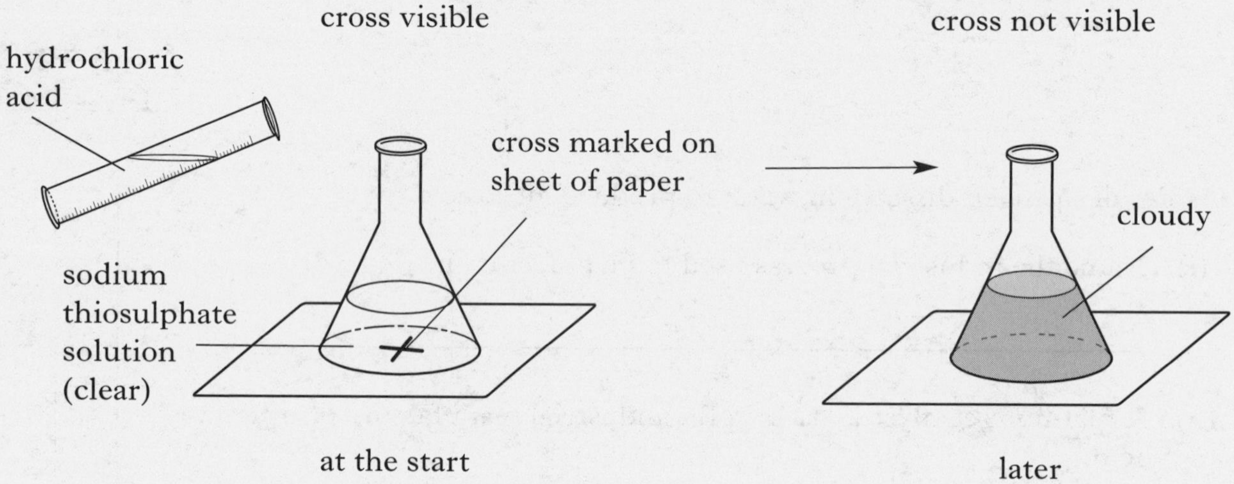

Her results are shown in the table.

Temperature/°C	Time/s
25	89
30	64
35	44
40	33
45	27
50	21

DO NOT WRITE IN THIS MARGIN

Marks KU PS

16. (*b*) (continued)

(i) Draw a line graph of the results.

Use appropriate scales to fill most of the graph paper.

(Additional graph paper, if required, will be found on page 27.)

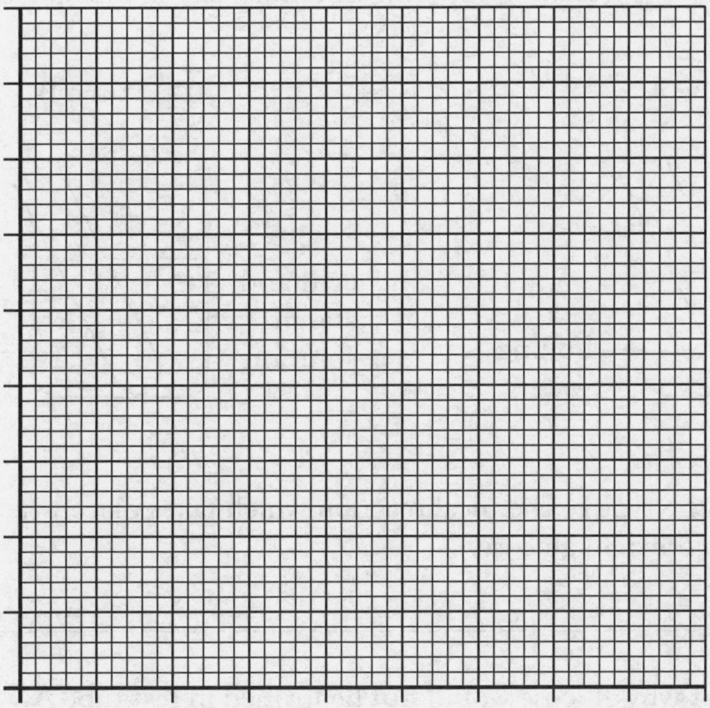

2

(ii) Use your graph to estimate the time taken, in seconds, for the cross to disappear at 60 °C.

____________________ **1**

(iii) Describe the relationship between the temperature and the **speed** of the reaction.

____

____________________ **1**

(*c*) State **one** factor that must be kept constant throughout this investigation.

____________________ **1**

(6)

[Turn over

DO NOT WRITE IN THIS MARGIN

Marks | KU | PS

17. Glucose and starch are both carbohydrates.

(*a*) Write the molecular formula for glucose.

______________________________ **1**

(*b*) A pupil set up the following experiment to turn starch into glucose.

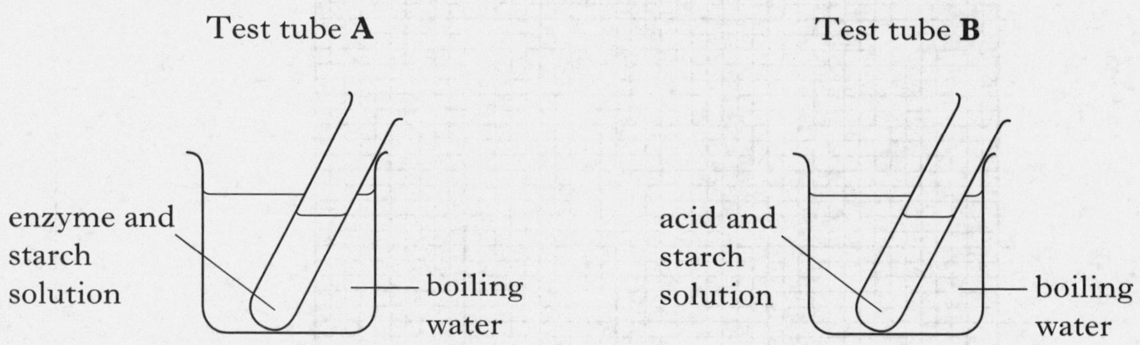

(i) Name the type of chemical reaction which takes place when starch is broken down to glucose.

______________________________ **1**

(ii) Suggest why glucose would **not** be formed in test tube **A**.

____

____

______________________________ **1**

(3)

DO NOT WRITE IN THIS MARGIN

Marks KU PS

18. Copper can be extracted from its oxide by heating copper(II) oxide with hydrogen gas. Water is also formed during the reaction.

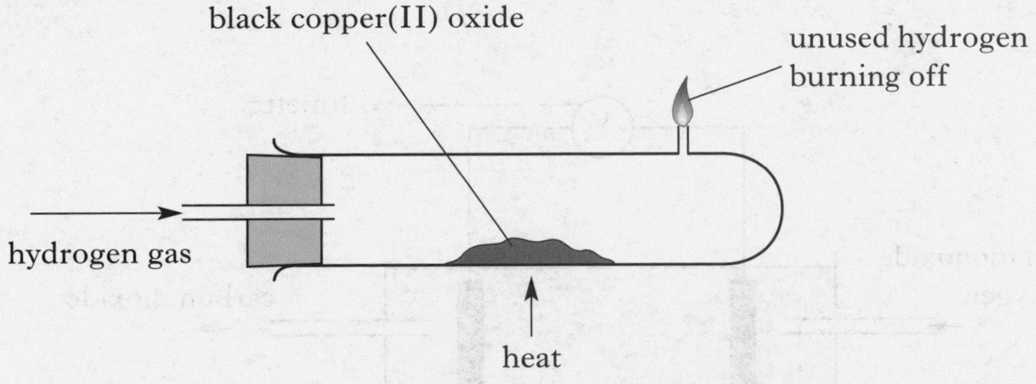

(*a*) Write an equation, using symbols and formulae, for the reaction between copper(II) oxide and hydrogen gas.
There is no need to balance the equation.

____ **1**

(*b*) Suggest the colour change which would be seen in the copper(II) oxide during the reaction.

____ **1**

(*c*) Suggest why calcium cannot be extracted from its oxide by heating with hydrogen gas.

____

____

____ **1**

(3)

[Turn over

DO NOT WRITE IN THIS MARGIN

	Marks	KU	PS

19. The cell below can be used in a carbon monoxide detector.

Carbon monoxide enters the cell along with oxygen from the air at electrode **A**.

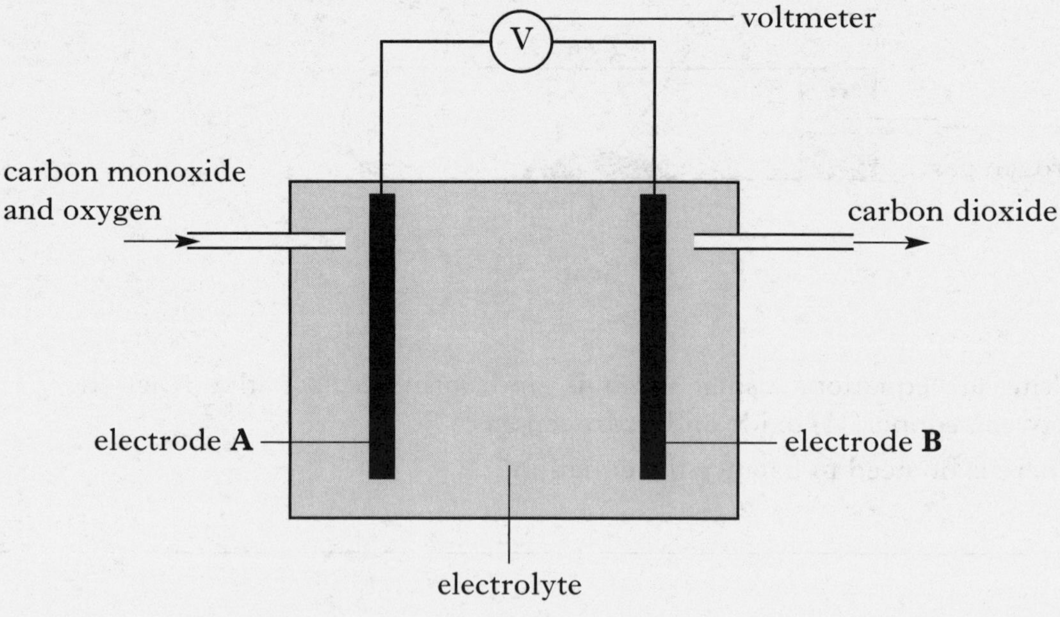

The reactions occurring at each electrode are:

Electrode A

$$CO(g) + H_2O(\ell) \longrightarrow CO_2(g) + 2H^+(aq) + 2e^-$$

Electrode B

$$2H^+(aq) + \tfrac{1}{2}O_2(g) + 2e^- \longrightarrow H_2O(\ell)$$

(*a*) **On the diagram**, clearly mark the path and direction of electron flow. **1**

(*b*) What is the purpose of the electrolyte in the above cell?

____

____ **1**

DO NOT WRITE IN THIS MARGIN

Marks KU PS

19. (continued)

(*c*) Sugar solution cannot be used as an electrolyte.
What does this indicate about the bonding in sugar?

____

____ **1**

(*d*) Platinum is used for the electrodes in this cell.

(i) To which family of metals does platinum belong?

____ **1**

(ii) Platinum is also used as a catalyst in a catalytic converter in car exhausts.
What does a catalytic converter do?

____

____

____ **1**

(5)

[Turn over

DO NOT WRITE IN THIS MARGIN

	Marks	KU	PS

20. Aluminium powder reacts with dilute sulphuric acid.

$$2Al(s) \quad + \quad 3H_2SO_4(aq) \longrightarrow Al_2(SO_4)_3(aq) \quad + \quad 3H_2(g)$$

(*a*) Circle the formula for the salt in the above equation. **1**

(*b*) Calculate the mass of hydrogen produced when 1·35 g of aluminium reacts with dilute sulphuric acid.

Answer ______________ g **2**

(3)

[*END OF QUESTION PAPER*]

DO NOT WRITE IN THIS MARGIN

KU	PS

ADDITIONAL SPACE FOR ANSWERS

ADDITIONAL GRAPH PAPER FOR QUESTION 16(*b*)(i)

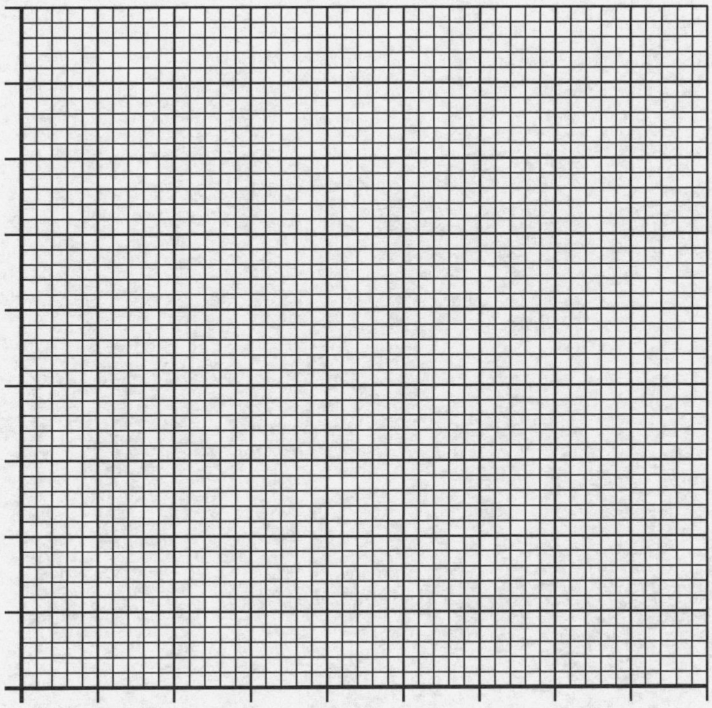

DO NOT WRITE IN THIS MARGIN

KU	PS

ADDITIONAL SPACE FOR ANSWERS

[BLANK PAGE]

FOR OFFICIAL USE

C

	KU	PS
Total Marks		

0500/402

NATIONAL QUALIFICATIONS 2006

MONDAY, 8 MAY
10.50 AM – 12.20 PM

CHEMISTRY
STANDARD GRADE
Credit Level

Fill in these boxes and read what is printed below.

Full name of centre

Town

Forename(s)

Surname

Date of birth
Day Month Year

Scottish candidate number

Number of seat

1 All questions should be attempted.

2 Necessary data will be found in the Data Booklet provided for Chemistry at Standard Grade and Intermediate 2.

3 The questions may be answered in any order but all answers are to be written in this answer book, and must be written clearly and legibly in ink.

4 Rough work, if any should be necessary, as well as the fair copy, is to be written in this book.
Rough work should be scored through when the fair copy has been written.

5 Additional space for answers and rough work will be found at the end of the book.

6 The size of the space provided for an answer should not be taken as an indication of how much to write. It is not necessary to use all the space.

7 Before leaving the examination room you must give this book to the invigilator. If you do not, you may lose all the marks for this paper.

SCOTTISH QUALIFICATIONS AUTHORITY

SA 0500/402 6/26770

PART 1

In Questions 1 to 7 of this part of the paper, an answer is given by circling the appropriate letter (or letters) in the answer grid provided.

In some questions, two letters are required for full marks.

If more than the correct number of answers is given, marks will be deducted.

A total of 20 marks is available in this part of the paper.

SAMPLE QUESTION

A CH_4	B H_2	C CO_2
D CO	E C_2H_5OH	F C

(*a*) Identify the hydrocarbon.

(A)	B	C
D	E	F

The one correct answer to part (*a*) is A. This should be circled.

(*b*) Identify the **two** elements.

A	(B)	C
D	E	(F)

As indicated in this question, there are **two** correct answers to part (*b*). These are B and F. Both answers are circled.

If, after you have recorded your answer, you decide that you have made an error and wish to make a change, you should cancel the original answer and circle the answer you now consider to be correct. Thus, in part (*a*), if you want to change an answer A to an answer D, your answer sheet would look like this:

~~(A)~~	B	C
(D)	E	F

If you want to change back to an answer which has already been scored out, you should enter a tick (✓) in the box of the answer of your choice, thus:

✓ ~~(A)~~	B	C
~~(D)~~	E	F

DO NOT WRITE IN THIS MARGIN

Marks | KU | PS

1. The grid shows the names of some metals.

A potassium	B platinum	C iron
D tin	E copper	F magnesium

(a) Identify the metal used as a catalyst in the Ostwald Process.

A	B	C
D	E	F

1

(b) Identify the metal produced in a Blast Furnace.

A	B	C
D	E	F

1

(c) Identify the metal which has a density of 8·92 g/cm^3.

You may wish to use the data booklet to help you.

A	B	C
D	E	F

1

(3)

[Turn over

DO NOT WRITE IN THIS MARGIN

Marks | KU | PS

2. The structures of some hydrocarbons are shown in the grid below.

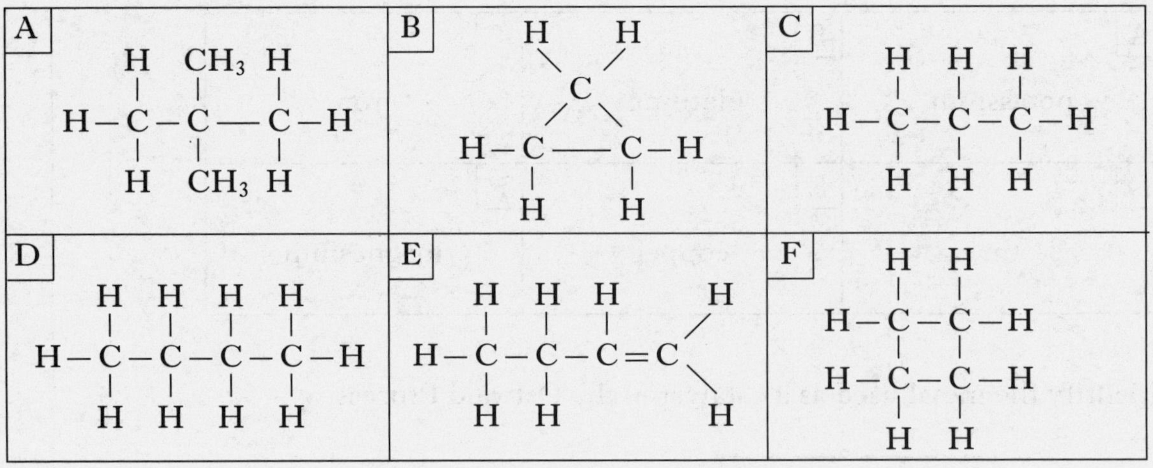

(*a*) Identify the **two** isomers.

A	B	C
D	E	F

1

(*b*) Identify the hydrocarbon which is the first member of a homologous series.

A	B	C
D	E	F

1

(2)

DO NOT WRITE IN THIS MARGIN

Marks KU PS

3. The grid shows the formulae for some gases.

A O_2	B N_2	C CO
D SO_2	E NO_2	F CO_2

(*a*) Identify the poisonous gas produced during the **incomplete combustion** of hydrocarbons.

A	B	C
D	E	F

1

(*b*) Identify the gas produced in air during a lightning storm.

A	B	C
D	E	F

1

(*c*) Identify the gas which is a reactant in the manufacture of ammonia (Haber Process).

A	B	C
D	E	F

1

(3)

[Turn over

DO NOT WRITE IN THIS MARGIN

Marks | KU | PS

4. The names of some oxides are shown in the grid.

A sodium oxide	B potassium oxide	C copper(II) oxide
D carbon dioxide	E zinc oxide	F sulphur dioxide

(*a*) Identify the **two** oxides which dissolve in water to form alkaline solutions.

A	B	C
D	E	F

1

(*b*) Identify the **two** oxides which are covalent.

A	B	C
D	E	F

1

(2)

DO NOT WRITE IN THIS MARGIN

Marks KU PS

5. The Periodic Table lists all known elements.

The grid shows the names of six common elements.

A oxygen	B calcium	C aluminium
D sodium	E magnesium	F fluorine

(*a*) Identify the **two** elements with similar chemical properties.

A	B	C
D	E	F

1

(*b*) Identify the element which can form ions with the same electron arrangement as argon.

A	B	C
D	E	F

1

(*c*) Identify the **two** elements which form an ionic compound with the formula of the type $\mathbf{XY_3}$, where **X** is the metal.

A	B	C
D	E	F

1

(3)

[Turn over

DO NOT WRITE IN THIS MARGIN

Marks | KU | PS

6. There are many different types of chemical reaction.

A precipitation	B hydrolysis	C oxidation
D neutralisation	E condensation	F addition

(*a*) Identify the type of chemical reaction that occurs when ethene reacts with hydrogen to form ethane.

A	B	C
D	E	F

1

(*b*) Identify the type of chemical reaction which occurs when a metal corrodes.

A	B	C
D	E	F

1

(*c*) Identify the **two** types of chemical reaction represented by the following equation.

$$Ba^{2+}(OH^-)_2(aq) + (H^+)_2SO_4^{2-}(aq) \longrightarrow Ba^{2+}SO_4^{2-}(s) + 2H_2O(\ell)$$

A	B	C
D	E	F

2

(4)

DO NOT WRITE IN THIS MARGIN

Marks | KU | PS

7. The grid shows pairs of chemicals.

A $CuO + C$	B $Na + H_2O$
C $Cu + NaNO_3$	D $C_5H_{12} + O_2$
E $Mg + H_2SO_4$	F $Ag + HCl$

(*a*) Which box contains a pair of chemicals that react to form water?

A	B
C	D
E	F

1

(*b*) Which **two** boxes contain pairs of chemicals that do **not** react together?

A	B
C	D
E	F

2

(3)

[Turn over

DO NOT WRITE IN THIS MARGIN

Marks KU PS

PART 2

A total of 40 marks is available in this part of the paper.

8. Teflon is the brand name for the plastic, poly(tetrafluoroethene).

The structure of part of a poly(tetrafluoroethene) molecule is shown below.

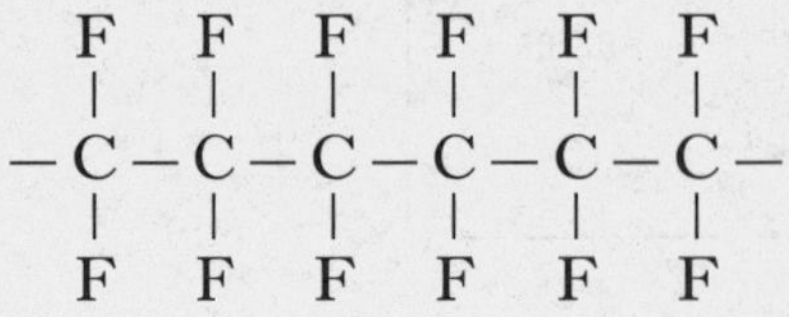

(*a*) Draw the full structural formula for the monomer used to make poly(tetrafluoroethene). **1**

(*b*) Teflon is a plastic which melts on heating.

What name is given to this type of plastic?

____ **1**

(2)

DO NOT WRITE IN THIS MARGIN

Marks | KU | PS

9. A sample of hydrogen was found to contain two different types of atom; ${}^{2}_{1}H$ and ${}^{1}_{1}H$.

(*a*) (i) What term is used to describe these different types of hydrogen atom?

____ **1**

(ii) This sample of hydrogen has an average atomic mass of 1·1.

What is the mass number of the most common type of atom in this sample of hydrogen?

____ **1**

(iii) Complete the table to show the number of protons and neutrons in each type of hydrogen atom.

Type of atom	**Number of protons**	**Number of neutrons**
${}^{2}_{1}\mathbf{H}$		
${}^{1}_{1}\mathbf{H}$		

1

(*b*) In a methane molecule (CH_4), hydrogen atoms form bonds with a carbon atom.

Draw a diagram to show the **shape** of a methane molecule.

1

(4)

[Turn over

DO NOT WRITE IN THIS MARGIN

Marks | KU | PS

10. A pupil set up the following experiment.

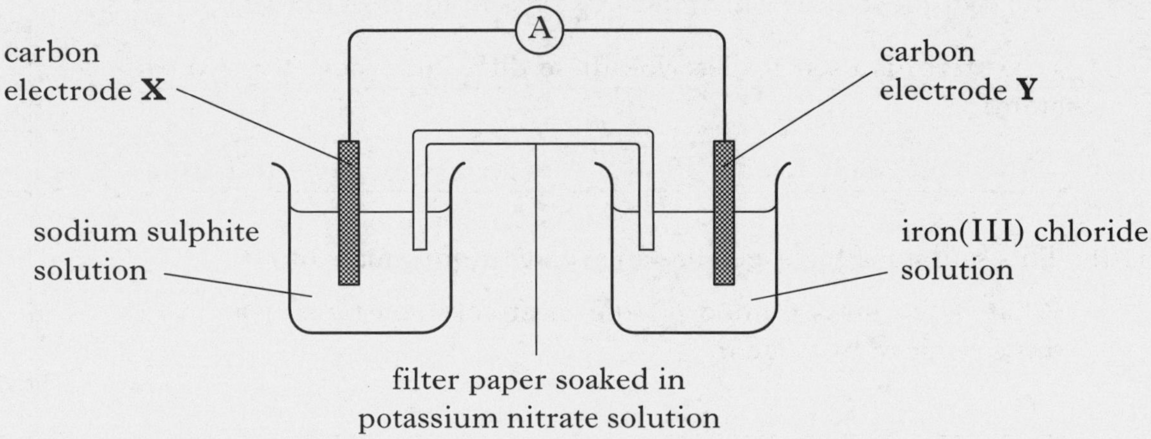

The reaction occurring at electrode **Y** is

$$Fe^{3+}(aq) + e^{-} \longrightarrow Fe^{2+}(aq)$$

(*a*) **On the diagram**, clearly mark the path and direction of electron flow. **1**

(*b*) Name the type of chemical reaction taking place at electrode **Y**.

____ **1**

(*c*) After some time, ferroxyl indicator was added to the beaker containing electrode **Y**.

What colour would the ferroxyl indicator turn?

______________________________ **1**

(3)

DO NOT WRITE IN THIS MARGIN

Marks KU PS

11. Some types of steel can rust.

(*a*) Name the **two** substances which must be present for steel to rust.

____ **1**

(*b*) Paint containing "Red Lead" (Pb_3O_4) was used to protect steel from rusting.

Calculate the percentage, by mass, of lead in "Red Lead".

__________ % **2**

(*c*) Stainless steel is a type of steel which does not need protection. It contains chromium which forms a layer of chromium(III) oxide on the steel.

Write the formula for chromium(III) oxide.

____ **1**

(4)

[Turn over

DO NOT WRITE IN THIS MARGIN

Marks KU PS

12. Laura added the catalyst manganese dioxide to hydrogen peroxide solution and measured the volume of oxygen produced.

$$2H_2O_2(aq) \longrightarrow 2H_2O\ (\ell) + O_2(g)$$

Her results are shown in the table.

Time/s	0	10	30	40	50	60
Volume of oxygen/cm³	0	25	35	38	40	40

(*a*) Draw a line graph of the results.

Use appropriate scales to fill most of the graph paper.

(Additional graph paper, if required, will be found on page 25.)

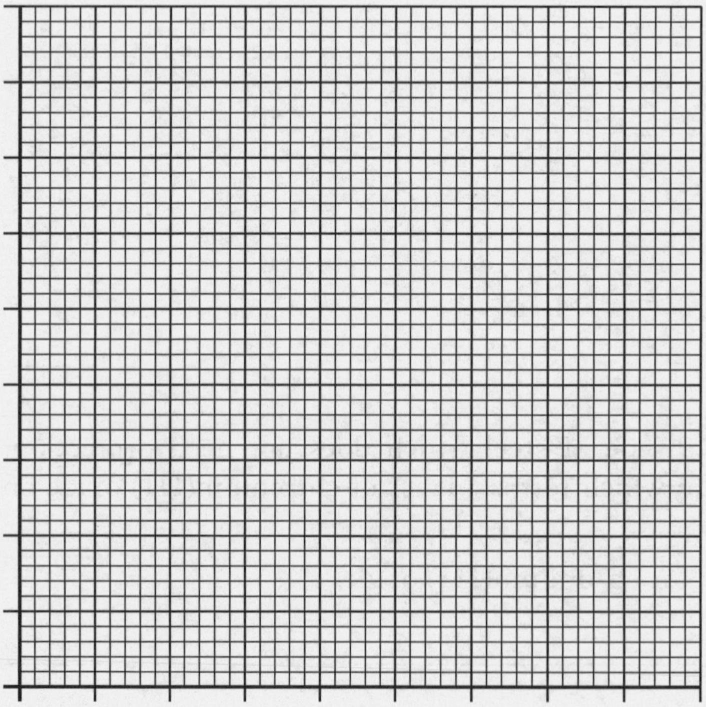

2

DO NOT WRITE IN THIS MARGIN

Marks | KU | PS

12. (continued)

(*b*) Using your graph, predict the volume of oxygen produced during the first 20 seconds.

_____________ cm^3 **1**

(*c*) Laura repeated the experiment at a higher temperature. She used the same volume and concentration of hydrogen peroxide solution.

Suggest a volume of oxygen produced during the first 30 seconds.

_____________ cm^3 **1**

(4)

[Turn over

DO NOT WRITE IN THIS MARGIN

Marks KU PS

13. Glucose is a carbohydrate.

(*a*) Name an isomer of glucose.

______________________________ **1**

(*b*) Glucose molecules join together to form starch in a polymerisation reaction.

Name the **type** of polymerisation reaction which takes place.

______________________________ **1**

(*c*) The diagram shows how glucose can be fermented to produce an alcohol. Carbon dioxide gas is also produced.

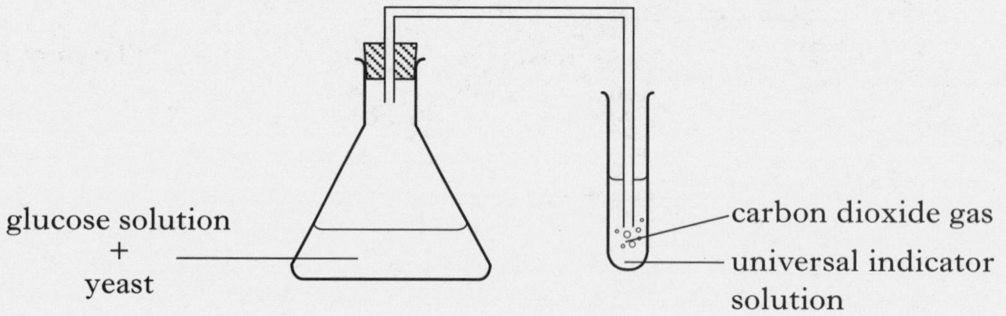

(i) What is the chemical name for the alcohol produced?

______________________________ **1**

(ii) Suggest the colour of the universal indicator solution after the carbon dioxide gas has been bubbled through it.

______________________________ **1**

(4)

DO NOT WRITE IN THIS MARGIN

Marks | KU | PS

14. Fuel cells produce electricity to power cars. The electricity is produced when hydrogen and oxygen react to form water.

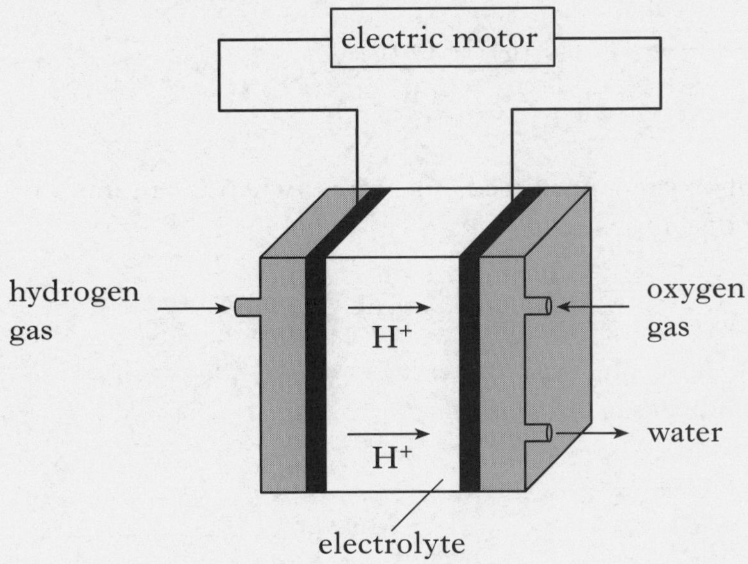

(*a*) Suggest a possible source of oxygen for use in the fuel cell.

______________________________ **1**

(*b*) Suggest an advantage in using fuel cells rather than petrol to power cars.

____

______________________________ **1**

(*c*) Write the ion-electron equation for the formation of hydrogen ions.

You may wish to use the data booklet to help you.

______________________________ **1**

(3)

[Turn over

DO NOT WRITE IN THIS MARGIN

Marks | KU | PS

15. Dinitrogen monoxide can be used to increase power in racing cars.

Dinitrogen monoxide decomposes to form nitrogen and oxygen.

$$2N_2O(g) \longrightarrow 2N_2(g) + O_2(g)$$

dinitrogen monoxide

(*a*) Calculate the mass of oxygen produced, in grams, when 22 grams of dinitrogen monoxide decomposes.

Answer ____________ g **2**

(*b*) Tom set up the following experiment to compare the time taken for the burning candles in gas jars **A** and **B** to go out.

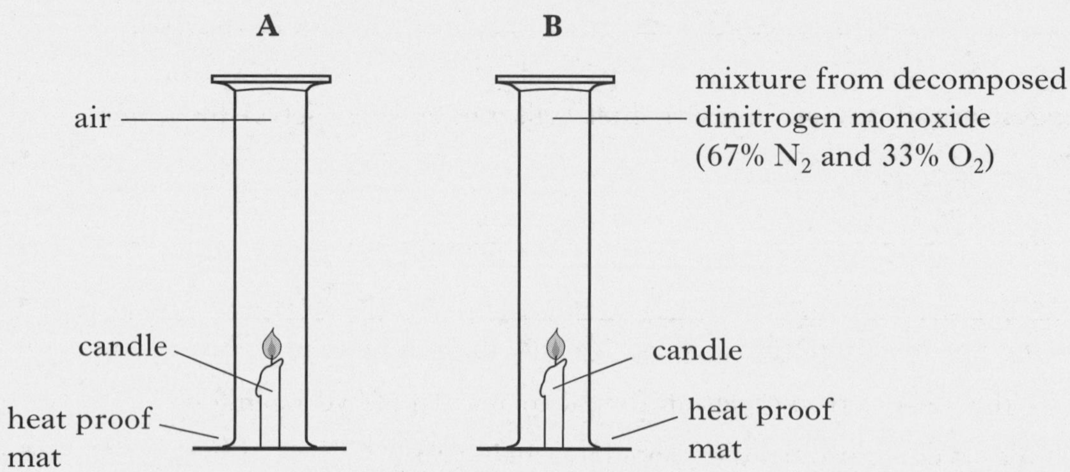

Circle the correct word in the table to show how the burning time of the candle in gas jar **B** compared to that in gas jar **A**.

Candle	Burning time/s
A	10
B	same/longer/shorter

1

(3)

DO NOT WRITE IN THIS MARGIN

	Marks	KU	PS

16. Ammonia gas is produced when barium hydroxide reacts with ammonium chloride.

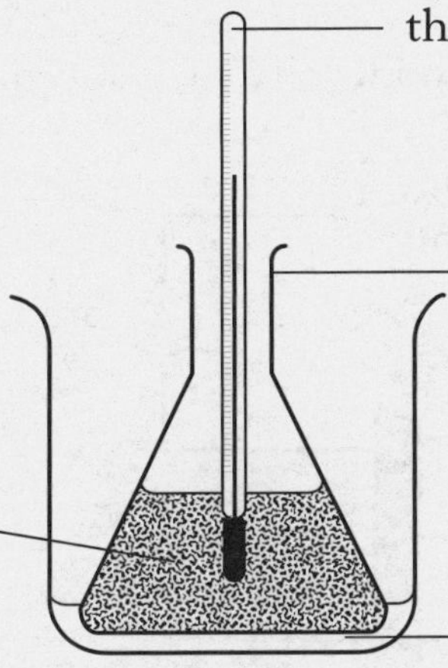

(*a*) The equation for the reaction which takes place is:

$Ba(OH)_2 \quad + \quad NH_4Cl \quad \rightarrow \quad NH_3 \quad + \quad BaCl_2 \quad + \quad H_2O$

Balance this equation. **1**

(*b*) Describe a test which would detect ammonia at the mouth of the flask.

____

____

____ **1**

(*c*) During the reaction the reading on the thermometer dropped from **25 °C** to **–5 °C.**

Suggest what would happen to the water in the beaker.

____

____

____ **1**

(3)

[Turn over

DO NOT WRITE IN THIS MARGIN

Marks | KU | PS

17. A class were given three chemicals labelled **X**, **Y** and **Z**.

The chemicals were glucose solution, copper chloride solution and dilute hydrochloric acid.

The apparatus below was used to help identify each solution.

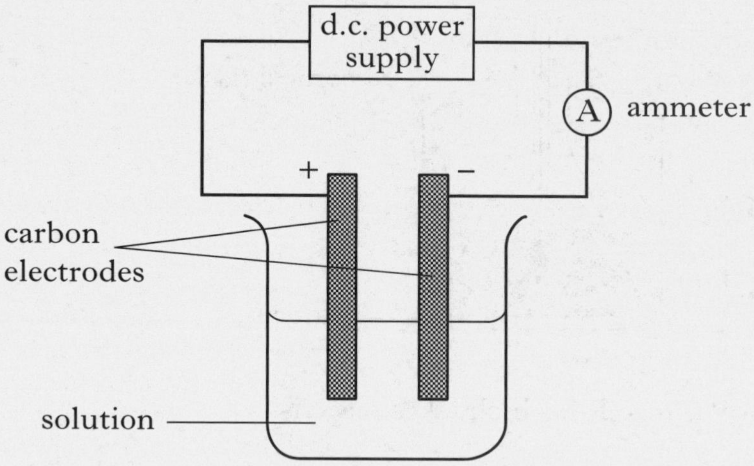

The class obtained the following results.

Solution	Ammeter reading	Observations at electrodes
X	Yes	bubbles of gas formed at both electrodes
Y	Yes	brown solid formed at negative electrode
Z	No	no reaction

(*a*) When electricity is passed through solutions **X** and **Y** they are broken up.

What term is used to describe this process?

____ **1**

DO NOT WRITE IN THIS MARGIN

Marks | KU | PS

17. (continued)

(*b*) (i) Identify **X**.

______________________ **1**

(ii) What type of bonding is present in **Z**?

______________________ **1**

(iii) Describe what was **seen** at the positive electrode when electricity was passed through solution **Y**.

______________________ **1**

(4)

[Turn over

DO NOT WRITE IN THIS MARGIN

Marks KU PS

18. A pupil carried out a titration experiment to find the concentration of a potassium hydroxide solution.

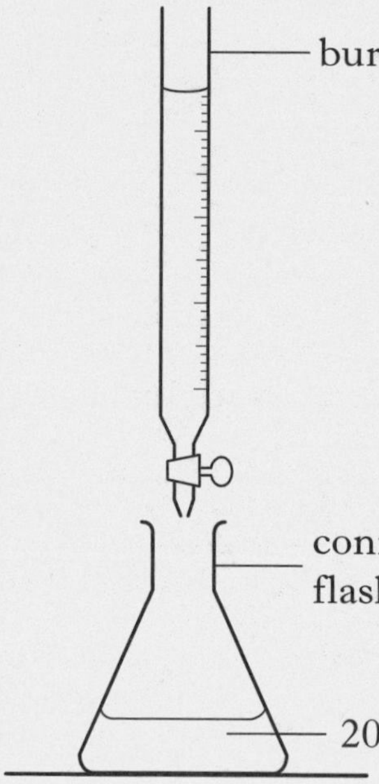

	Rough titre	1st titre	2nd titre
Initial burette reading/cm^3	0·5	16·8	32·3
Final burette reading/cm^3	16·8	32·3	48·0
Volume used/cm^3	16·3	15·5	15·7

The equation for the reaction is:

$$KOH(aq) + HCl(aq) \longrightarrow KCl(aq) + H_2O(\ell)$$

(*a*) Using the results in the table, calculate the **average** volume of hydrochloric acid required to neutralise the potassium hydroxide solution.

____________ cm^3 **1**

DO NOT WRITE IN THIS MARGIN

Marks KU PS

18. (continued)

(*b*) Use the pupil's results to calculate the concentration, in mol/l, of the potassium hydroxide solution.

Show your working clearly.

_______________ mol/l **2**

(*c*) The indicator was removed from the potassium chloride solution by filtering the solution through charcoal.

How would the pupil then obtain a sample of **solid** potassium chloride from the solution?

____

____

____

_______________ **1**

(4)

[Turn over

DO NOT WRITE IN THIS MARGIN

Marks | KU | PS

19. Esters are compounds used in perfumes.

Esters can be made when an alcohol reacts with a carboxylic acid.

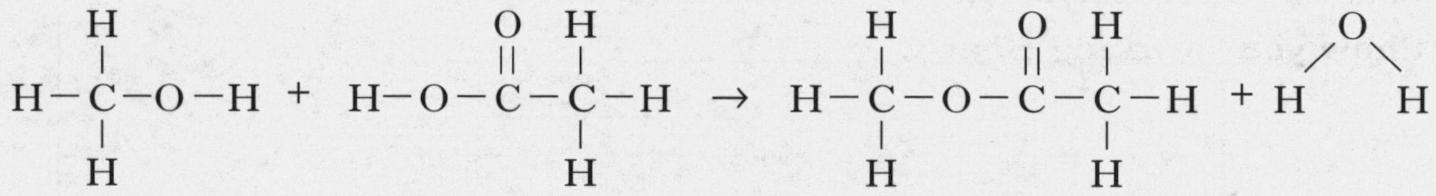

alcohol carboxylic acid ester water

(*a*) Draw the **full** structural formula for the **ester** produced in the following reaction.

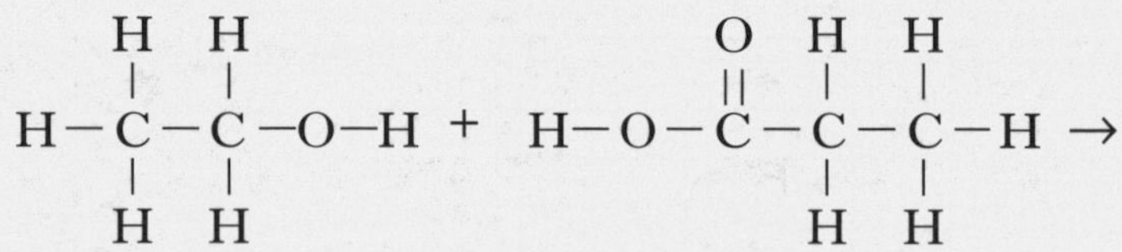

alcohol carboxylic acid

1

(*b*) After some time the esters in perfumes react with water and break down to form the alcohol and carboxylic acid again.

Suggest a name for the type of chemical reaction taking place.

____ **1**

(2)

[*END OF QUESTION PAPER*]

DO NOT WRITE IN THIS MARGIN

KU	PS

ADDITIONAL SPACE FOR ANSWERS

ADDITIONAL GRAPH PAPER FOR QUESTION 12(*a*)

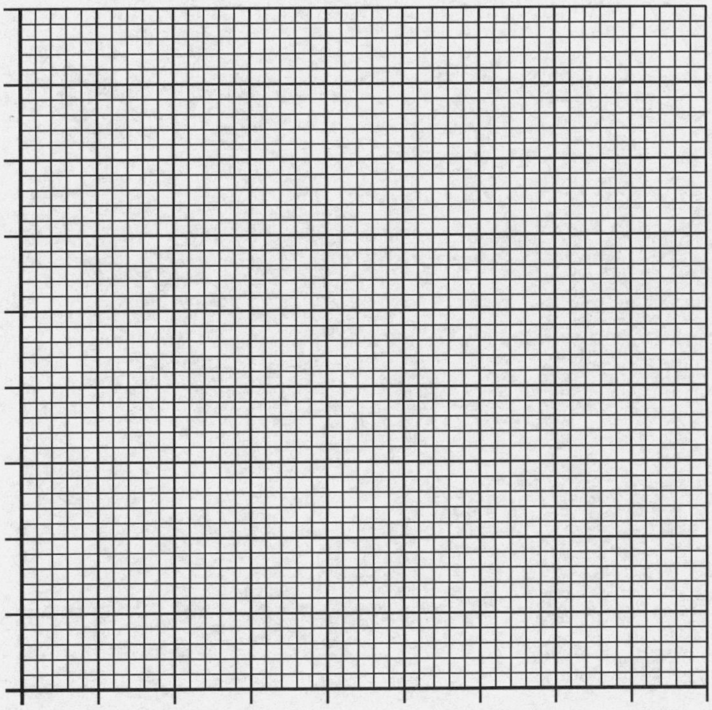

DO NOT WRITE IN THIS MARGIN

KU	PS

ADDITIONAL SPACE FOR ANSWERS

2007 | Credit

[BLANK PAGE]

FOR OFFICIAL USE

C

	KU	PS
Total Marks		

0500/402

NATIONAL QUALIFICATIONS 2007

THURSDAY, 10 MAY
10.50 AM – 12.20 PM

CHEMISTRY
STANDARD GRADE
Credit Level

Fill in these boxes and read what is printed below.

Full name of centre

Town

Forename(s)

Surname

Date of birth

Day Month Year

Scottish candidate number

Number of seat

1 All questions should be attempted.
2 Necessary data will be found in the Data Booklet provided for Chemistry at Standard Grade and Intermediate 2.
3 The questions may be answered in any order but all answers are to be written in this answer book, and must be written clearly and legibly in ink.
4 Rough work, if any should be necessary, as well as the fair copy, is to be written in this book.
Rough work should be scored through when the fair copy has been written.
5 Additional space for answers and rough work will be found at the end of the book.
6 The size of the space provided for an answer should not be taken as an indication of how much to write. It is not necessary to use all the space.
7 Before leaving the examination room you must give this book to the invigilator. If you do not, you may lose all the marks for this paper.

SCOTTISH QUALIFICATIONS AUTHORITY

PART 1

In Questions 1 to 9 of this part of the paper, an answer is given by circling the appropriate letter (or letters) in the answer grid provided.

In some questions, two letters are required for full marks.

If more than the correct number of answers is given, marks will be deducted.

A total of 20 marks is available in this part of the paper.

SAMPLE QUESTION

A CH_4	B H_2	C CO_2
D CO	E C_2H_5OH	F C

(*a*) Identify the hydrocarbon.

(A)	B	C
D	E	F

The one correct answer to part (*a*) is A. This should be circled.

(*b*) Identify the **two** elements.

A	(B)	C
D	E	(F)

As indicated in this question, there are **two** correct answers to part (*b*). These are B and F. Both answers are circled.

If, after you have recorded your answer, you decide that you have made an error and wish to make a change, you should cancel the original answer and circle the answer you now consider to be correct. Thus, in part (*a*), if you want to change an answer A to an answer D, your answer sheet would look like this:

~~(A)~~	B	C
(D)	E	F

If you want to change back to an answer which has already been scored out, you should enter a tick (✓) in the box of the answer of your choice, thus:

✓ ~~(A)~~	B	C
~~(D)~~	E	F

DO NOT WRITE IN THIS MARGIN

Marks KU PS

1.

Testing gases

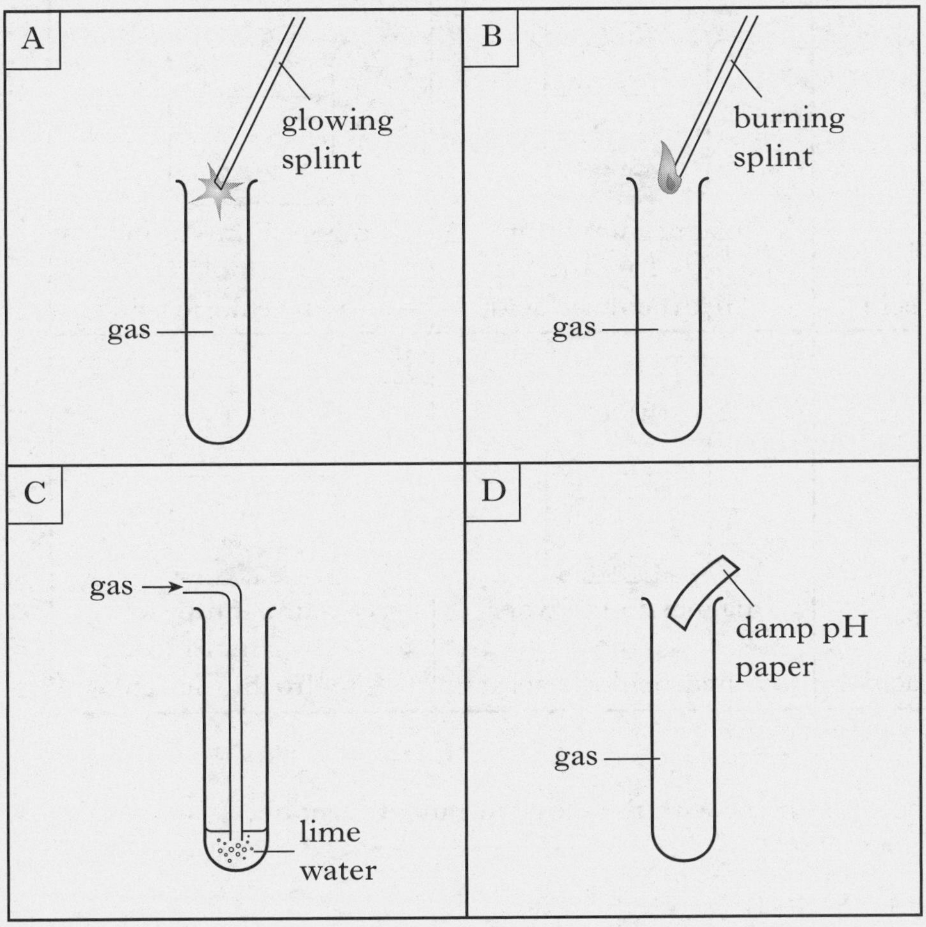

(*a*) Identify the test for oxygen gas.

A	B
C	D

1

(*b*) Identify a test for ammonia gas.

A	B
C	D

1

(2)

[Turn over

DO NOT WRITE IN THIS MARGIN

Marks KU PS

2. Zinc and magnesium both react with dilute hydrochloric acid.

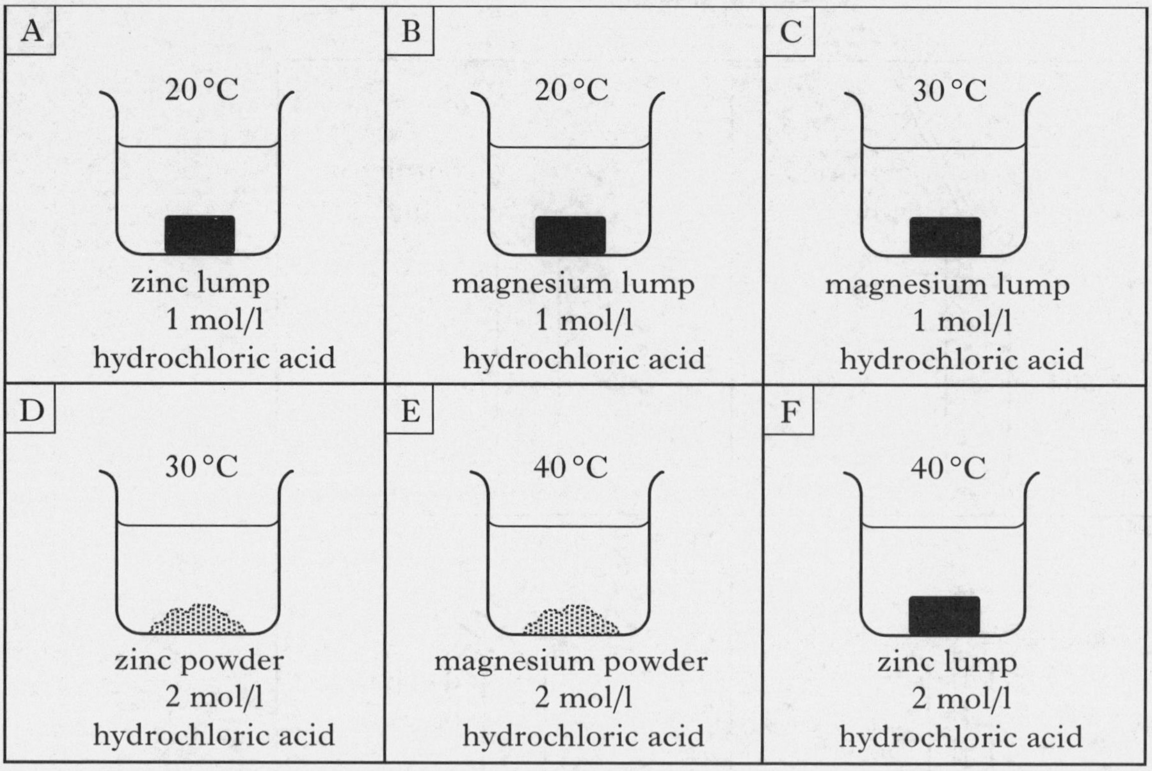

(*a*) Identify the experiment with the **slowest** rate of reaction.

A	B	C
D	E	F

1

(*b*) Identify the **two** experiments which could be used to investigate the effect of temperature on the rate of reaction.

A	B	C
D	E	F

1

(2)

DO NOT WRITE IN THIS MARGIN

Marks KU PS

3. Distillation of crude oil produces several fractions.

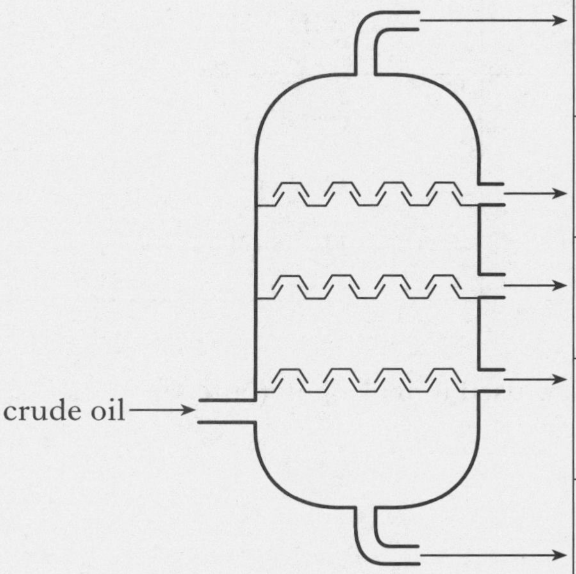

Fraction	***Number of carbon atoms per molecule***
A	1–4
B	4–10
C	10–16
D	16–20
E	20+

(*a*) Identify the fraction which is used to tar roads.

A
B
C
D
E

1

(*b*) Identify the fraction with the lowest boiling point.

A
B
C
D
E

1

(2)

[Turn over

DO NOT WRITE IN THIS MARGIN

Marks KU PS

4. The structural formulae for some hydrocarbons are shown below.

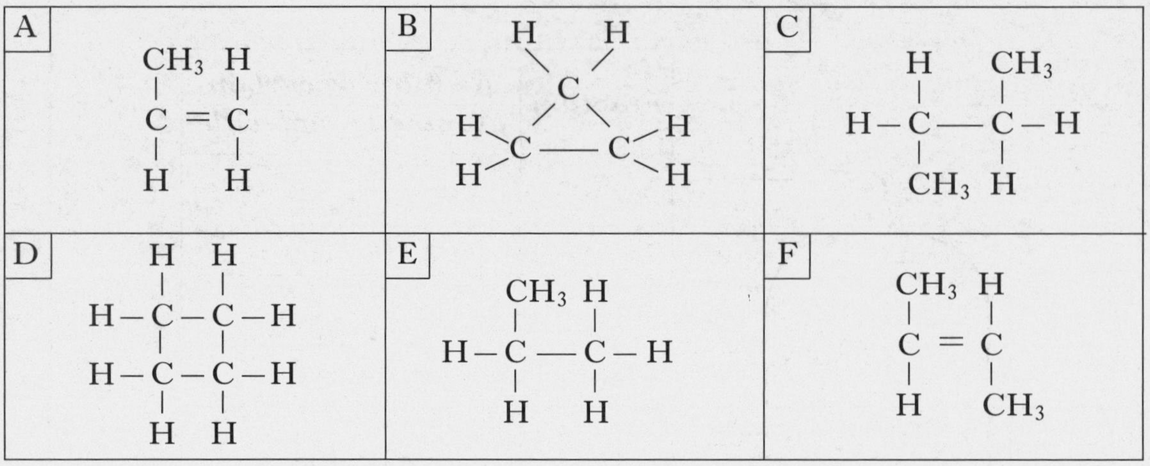

(*a*) Identify the hydrocarbon which could be used to make poly(butene).

A	B	C
D	E	F

1

(*b*) Identify the **two** hydrocarbons with the general formula C_nH_{2n} which do **not** react quickly with hydrogen.

A	B	C
D	E	F

1

(2)

DO NOT WRITE IN THIS MARGIN

Marks KU PS

5. The table contains information about some substances.

Substance	***Melting point/ °C***	***Boiling point/ °C***	***Conducts as a solid***	***Conducts as a liquid***
A	1700	2230	no	no
B	605	1305	no	yes
C	−13	77	no	no
D	801	1413	no	yes
E	181	1347	yes	yes
F	−39	357	yes	yes

(*a*) Identify the substance which exists as covalent molecules.

A
B
C
D
E
F

1

(*b*) Identify the metal which is liquid at 25 °C.

A
B
C
D
E
F

1

(2)

[Turn over

DO NOT WRITE IN THIS MARGIN

Marks KU PS

6. Equations are used to represent chemical reactions.

A	$Sn(s) \longrightarrow Sn^{2+}(aq) + 2e^-$
B	$Cu^{2+}(aq) + 2e^- \longrightarrow Cu(s)$
C	$H^+(aq) + OH^-(aq) \longrightarrow H_2O(\ell)$
D	$2Mg(s) + O_2(g) \longrightarrow 2MgO(s)$
E	$SO_2(g) + H_2O(\ell) \longrightarrow 2H^+(aq) + SO_3^{2-}(aq)$

(*a*) Identify the equation which represents the formation of acid rain.

A
B
C
D
E

1

(*b*) Identify the equation which represents neutralisation.

A
B
C
D
E

1

(*c*) Identify the **two** equations in which a substance is oxidised.

A
B
C
D
E

2

(4)

DO NOT WRITE IN THIS MARGIN

Marks KU PS

7. A student made some statements about the particles found in atoms.

A	It has a positive charge.
B	It has a negative charge.
C	It has a relative mass of almost zero.
D	It has a relative mass of 1.
E	It is found inside the nucleus.
F	It is found outside the nucleus.

Identify the **two** statements which apply to **both** a proton and a neutron.

A
B
C
D
E
F

(2)

8. A student made some statements about the reaction of silver(I) oxide with excess dilute hydrochloric acid.

A	The concentration of hydrogen ions increases.
B	Carbon dioxide gas is produced.
C	An insoluble salt is produced.
D	Hydrogen gas is produced.
E	Water is produced.

Identify the **two** correct statements.

A
B
C
D
E

(2)

DO NOT WRITE IN THIS MARGIN

Marks KU PS

9. When two different electrodes are joined in a cell, a chemical reaction takes place and a voltage is produced.

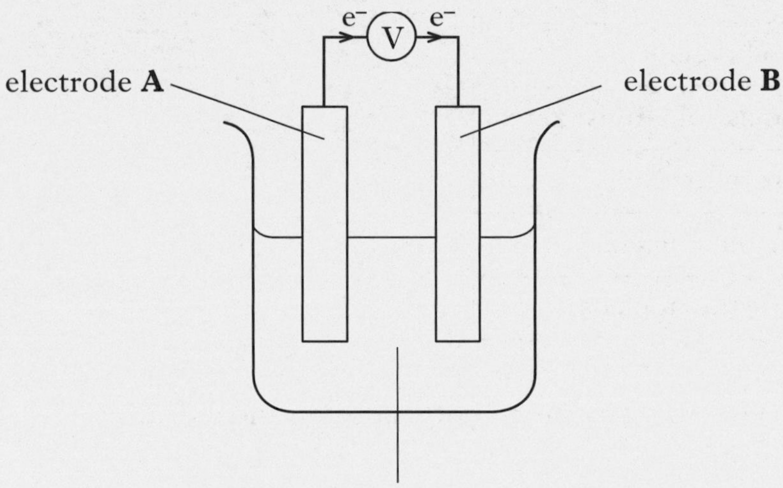

sodium chloride solution and ferroxyl indicator

	Electrode A	*Electrode B*
A	magnesium	iron
B	iron	carbon
C	iron	aluminium
D	iron	copper
E	lead	iron

Which **two** pairs of electrodes will produce a flow of electrons in the same direction as shown in the diagram and would produce a blue colour around electrode **A**?

You may wish to use the data booklet to help you.

A
B
C
D
E

(2)

[Turn over for Part 2 on *Page twelve*

DO NOT WRITE IN THIS MARGIN

Marks | KU | PS

PART 2

A total of 40 marks is available in this part of the paper.

10. A sample of silver was found to contain two isotopes, $^{107}_{47}Ag$ and $^{109}_{47}Ag$.

(*a*) This sample of silver has an average atomic mass of 108.

What does this indicate about the amount of each isotope in this sample?

____

____ **1**

(*b*) Complete the table to show the number of each type of particle in a $^{107}_{47}Ag^{+}$ ion.

Particle	***Number***
proton	
neutron	
electron	

2

(*c*) Silver can be displaced from a solution of silver(I) nitrate.

$$AgNO_3(aq) \quad + \quad Cu(s) \quad \longrightarrow \quad Ag(s) \quad + \quad Cu(NO_3)_2(aq)$$

(i) Balance this equation. **1**

(ii) Name a metal which would **not** displace silver from silver(I) nitrate.

You may wish to use the data booklet to help you.

____ **1**

(5)

DO NOT WRITE IN THIS MARGIN

Marks KU PS

11. Alkanoic acids are a family of compounds which contain the 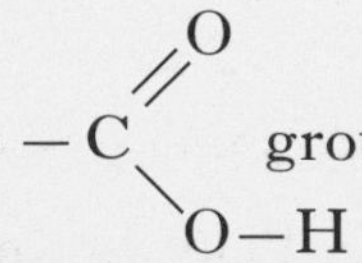 group.

The **full** structural formulae for the first three members are shown.

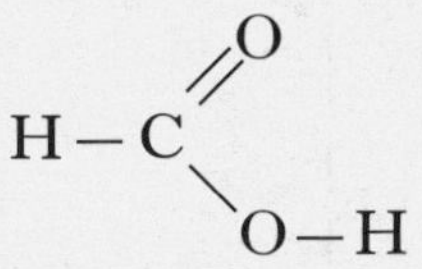

methanoic acid

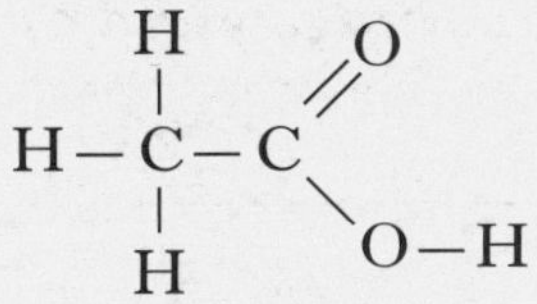

ethanoic acid

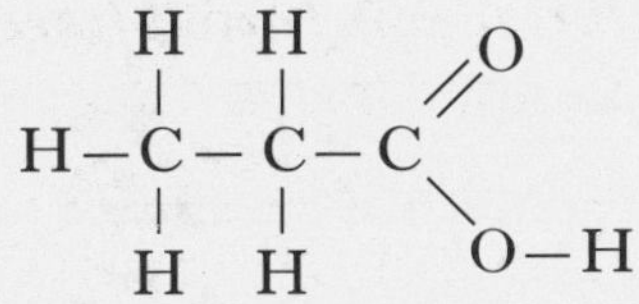

propanoic acid

(*a*) Draw the **full** structural formula for the alkanoic acid containing 4 carbon atoms. **1**

(*b*) The table gives information on some alkanoic acids.

Acid	*Boiling point/ °C*
methanoic acid	101
ethanoic acid	118
propanoic acid	141
butanoic acid	164

(i) Using this information, make a general statement linking the boiling point to the number of carbon atoms.

____

____

____ **1**

(ii) Predict the boiling point of pentanoic acid.

____________ °C **1**

(3)

[Turn over

DO NOT WRITE IN THIS MARGIN

Marks KU PS

12. Ammonia is made when nitrogen and hydrogen react together.

The table below shows the percentage yields obtained when nitrogen and hydrogen react at different pressures.

Pressure/atmospheres	***Percentage yield of ammonia***
25	28
50	40
100	53
200	67
400	80

(*a*) Draw a line graph of percentage yield against pressure.

Use appropriate scales to fill most of the graph paper.

(Additional graph paper, if required, will be found on page 27.)

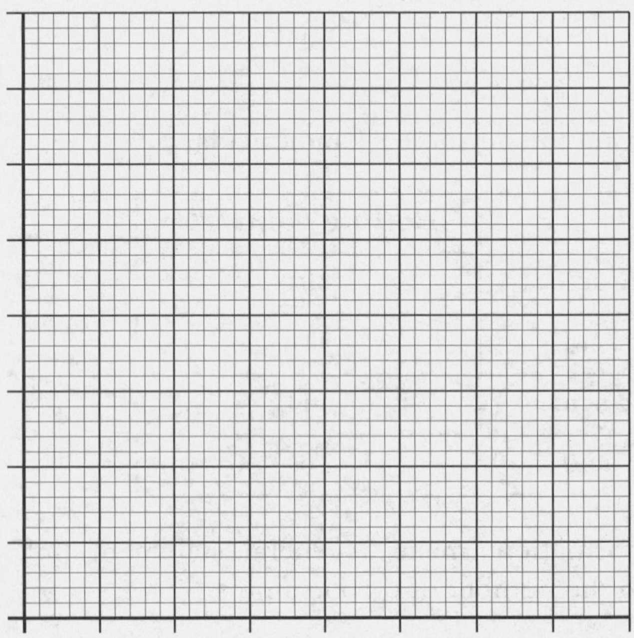

2

(*b*) Use your graph to estimate the percentage yield of ammonia at 150 atmospheres.

____ **1**

DO NOT WRITE IN THIS MARGIN

Marks KU PS

12. (continued)

(*c*) Ammonia can be produced in the lab by heating an ammonium compound with soda lime.

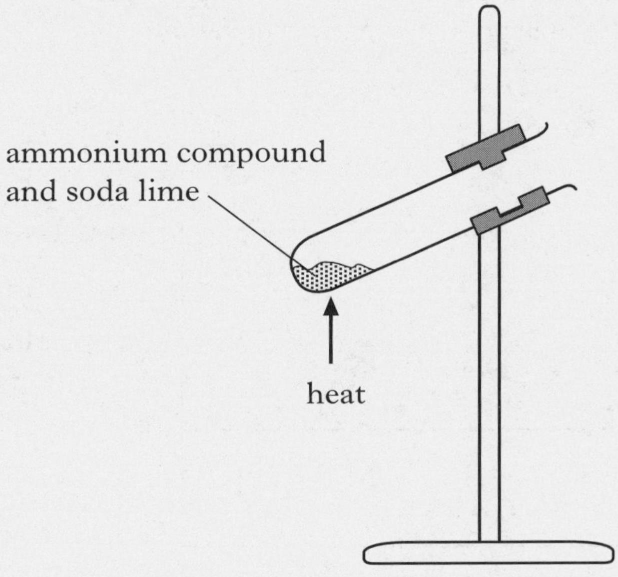

In order to produce ammonia, what **type** of compound must soda lime be?

______________________________ 1

(4)

[Turn over

Marks | KU | PS

13. Starch and sucrose can be hydrolysed to produce simple sugars.

Chromatography is a technique which can be used to identify the sugars produced.

Samples of known sugar solutions are spotted on the base line. The solvent travels up the paper carrying spots of sugars at different rates.

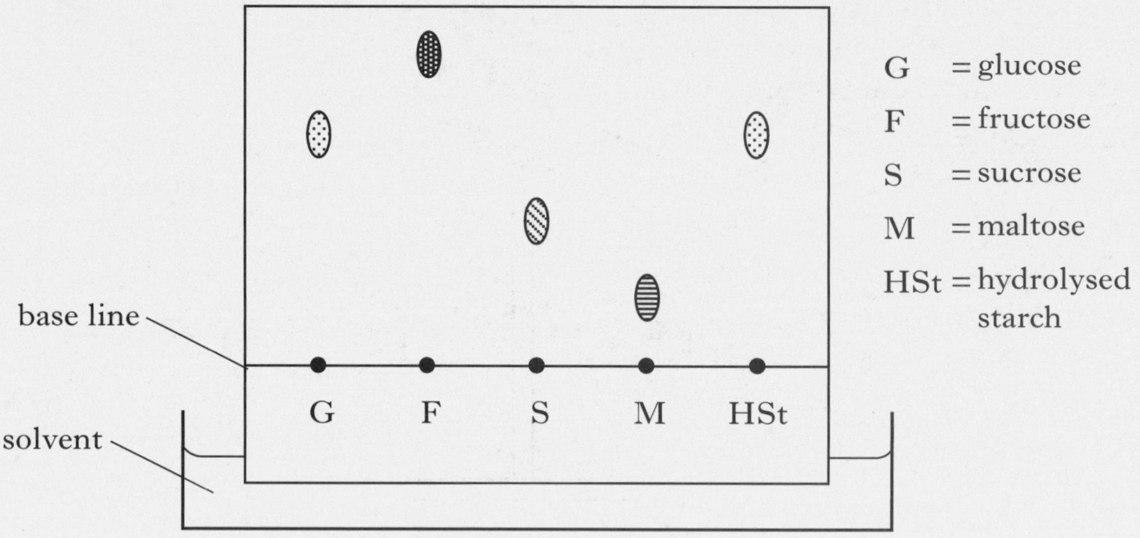

The diagram above shows that **only glucose** is produced when starch is hydrolysed.

(*a*) The chromatogram below can be used to identify the simple sugars produced when sucrose is hydrolysed.

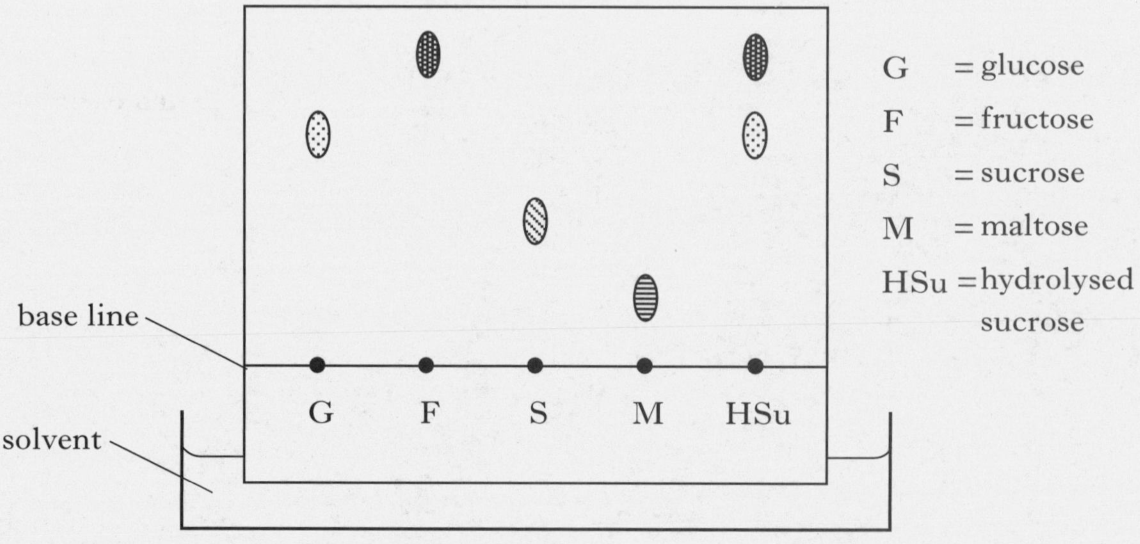

Name the sugars produced when sucrose is hydrolysed.

____ **1**

DO NOT WRITE IN THIS MARGIN

Marks KU PS

13. (continued)

(*b*) What **type** of substance, present in the digestive system, acts as a catalyst in the hydrolysis of sucrose?

____ **1**

(2)

[Turn over

DO NOT WRITE IN THIS MARGIN

Marks KU PS

14. Cars made from steel can be protected from rusting in a number of ways.

(*a*) Circle the correct word to complete the sentence below.

Steel does not rust when attached to the {negative / positive} terminal of a car battery. **1**

(*b*) The steel body of the car can be coated by dipping it in molten zinc.

(i) What name is given to this process?

____ **1**

(ii) Explain why the steel does **not** rust even when the zinc coating is scratched.

____

____

____ **1**

(3)

DO NOT WRITE IN THIS MARGIN

Marks KU PS

15. The atoms in a chlorine molecule are held together by a covalent bond. A covalent bond is a shared pair of electrons.

The chlorine molecule can be represented as

● = electron

(*a*) Showing **all** outer electrons, draw a similar diagram to represent a molecule of hydrogen chloride, HCl. **1**

(*b*) In forming covalent bonds, why do atoms share electrons?

____

____

____ **1**

(2)

[Turn over

DO NOT WRITE IN THIS MARGIN

Marks KU PS

16. Ethanol is the alcohol found in alcoholic drinks.

It can be produced as shown in the diagram.

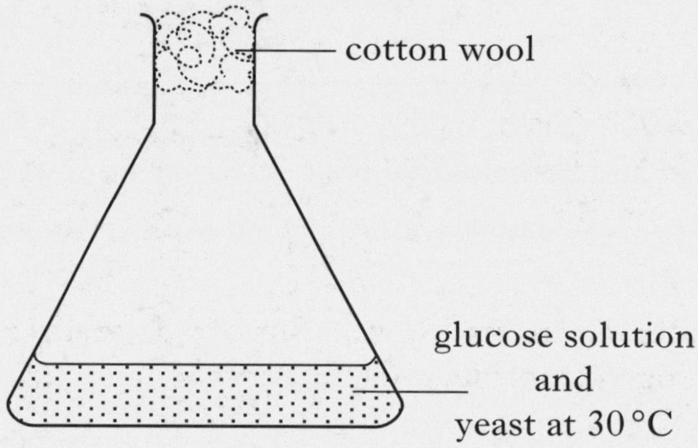

(*a*) (i) Name the type of chemical reaction taking place in the flask.

____ **1**

(ii) What would happen to the rate of the reaction if the experiment above was repeated at 50 °C?

____ **1**

(*b*) In industry, alcohols can be produced from alkenes as shown in the example below.

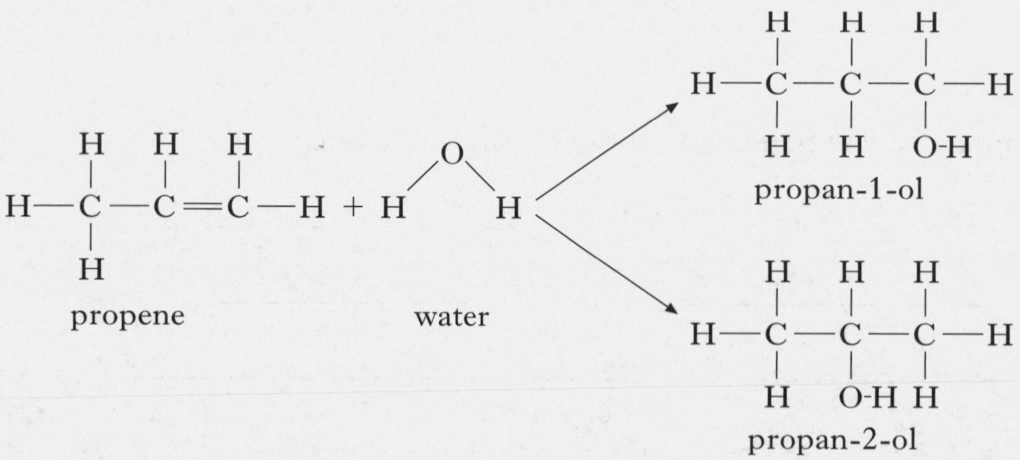

(i) Name the type of chemical reaction taking place.

____ **1**

DO NOT WRITE IN THIS MARGIN

Marks	KU	PS

16. (*b*) (continued)

(ii) What **term** is used to describe a pair of alcohols like propan-1-ol and propan-2-ol?

____ **1**

(iii) Propan-1-ol and propan-2-ol have different boiling points.

Name the process which could be used to separate a mixture of these alcohols.

____ **1**

(5)

[Turn over

DO NOT WRITE IN THIS MARGIN

Marks | KU | PS

17. The table contains information on minerals.

Mineral	*Formula*
cinnabar	HgS
fluorite	CaF_2
gibbsite	$Al(OH)_3$
haematite	Fe_2O_3
zinc blende	ZnS

(*a*) State the chemical name for zinc blende.

____ **1**

(*b*) Name the salt formed when gibbsite reacts with dilute hydrochloric acid.

____ **1**

(*c*) Calculate the percentage, by mass, of calcium in fluorite (CaF_2).

Show your working clearly.

__________ % **2**

(*d*) Iron metal can be extracted from haematite (Fe_2O_3) by heating with carbon monoxide. Carbon dioxide is also produced.

Write an equation, using **symbols** and **formulae**, for this reaction.

There is no need to balance it.

____ **1**

(*e*) Name a metal which can be extracted from its ore by heat alone.

____ **1**

(6)

DO NOT WRITE IN THIS MARGIN

Marks KU PS

18. Nylon is a polymer with many uses.

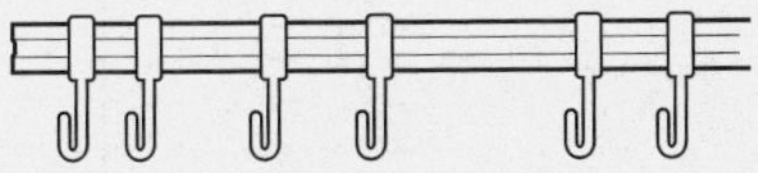

curtain rail

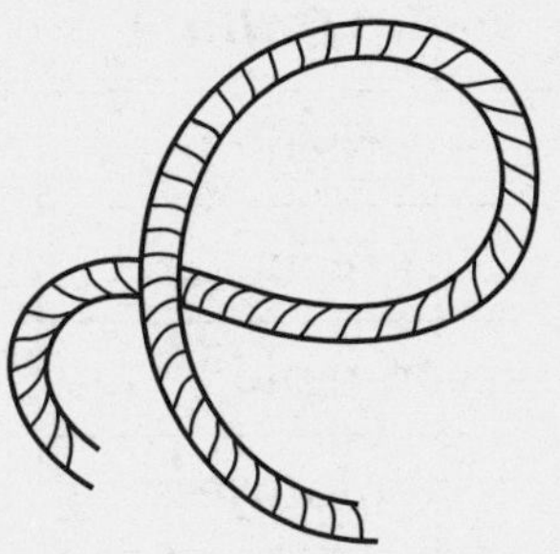

rope

jacket

(*a*) Nylon is a thermoplastic polymer.

What does thermoplastic mean?

____

____ **1**

(*b*) Nylon is a polymer made from two different monomers as shown.

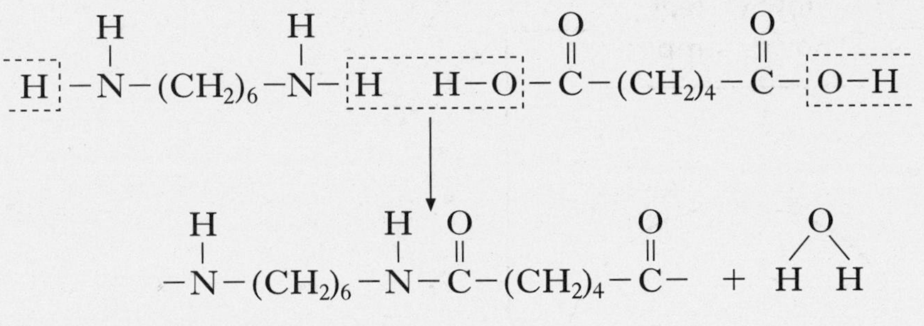

nylon

During the polymerisation reaction, water is also produced.

Suggest a name for this **type** of polymerisation.

____ **1**

(2)

[Turn over

DO NOT WRITE IN THIS MARGIN

Marks KU PS

19. Many ionic compounds are coloured.

Compound	***Colour***
nickel(II) nitrate	green
nickel(II) sulphate	green
potassium permanganate	purple
potassium sulphate	colourless

(*a*) Using the information in the table, state the colour of the potassium ion.

____ **1**

(*b*) Write the **ionic** formula for nickel(II) nitrate.

____ **1**

(*c*) A student set up the following experiment to investigate the colour of the ions in copper(II) chromate.

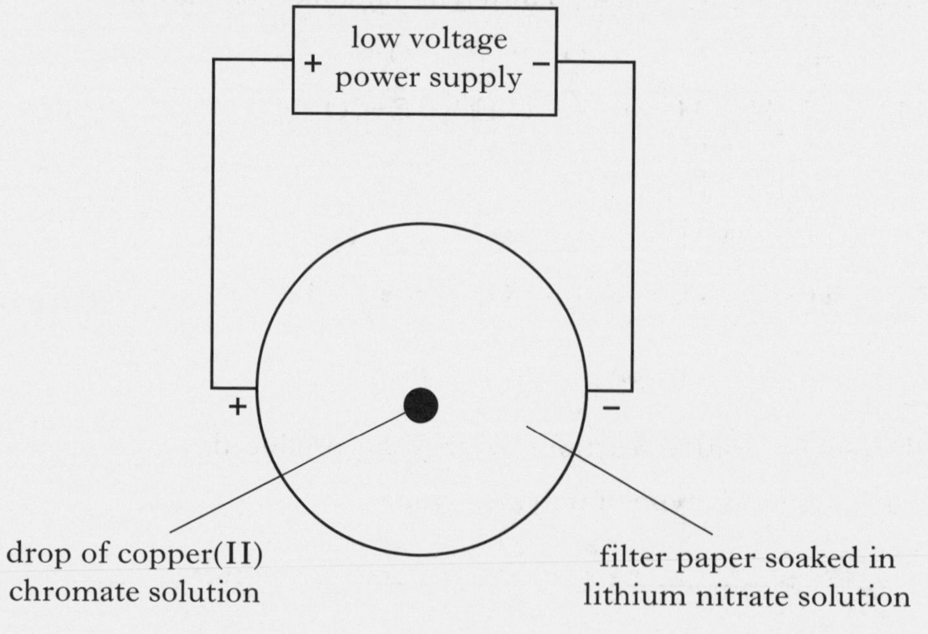

The student made the following observation.

Observation
yellow colour moves to the positive electrode
blue colour moves to the negative electrode

DO NOT WRITE IN THIS MARGIN

Marks KU PS

19. **(*c*) (continued)**

(i) State the colour of the chromate ion.

______________________________ **1**

(ii) Lithium nitrate solution is used as the electrolyte.

What is the purpose of an electrolyte?

____

____

______________________________ **1**

(iii) Suggest why lithium phosphate can **not** be used as the electrolyte in this experiment.

You may wish to use the data booklet to help you.

____

____

______________________________ **1**

(5)

[Turn over

DO NOT WRITE IN THIS MARGIN

Marks KU PS

20. Indigestion is caused by excess acid in the stomach. Indigestion remedies containing calcium carbonate neutralise some of this acid.

Christine carried out an experiment to find the mass of calcium carbonate required to neutralise a dilute hydrochloric acid solution.

She added calcium carbonate until all the acid had been used up.

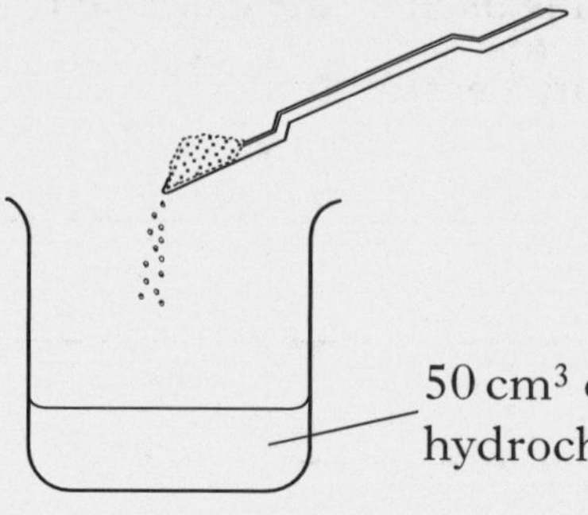

(*a*) Calculate the number of moles of dilute hydrochloric acid used in the experiment.

________________ mol **1**

(*b*) The equation for the reaction is

$$CaCO_3(s) + 2HCl(aq) \longrightarrow CaCl_2(aq) + H_2O(\ell) + CO_2(g)$$

(i) Using your answer from part (*a*), calculate the number of moles of calcium carbonate required to neutralise the dilute hydrochloric acid.

________________ mol **1**

(ii) Using your answer from part (*b*)(i), calculate the **mass** of calcium carbonate ($CaCO_3$) required to neutralise the acid.

________________ g **1**

(3)

[*END OF QUESTION PAPER*]

DO NOT WRITE IN THIS MARGIN

KU	PS

ADDITIONAL SPACE FOR ANSWERS

ADDITIONAL GRAPH PAPER FOR QUESTION 12(*a*)

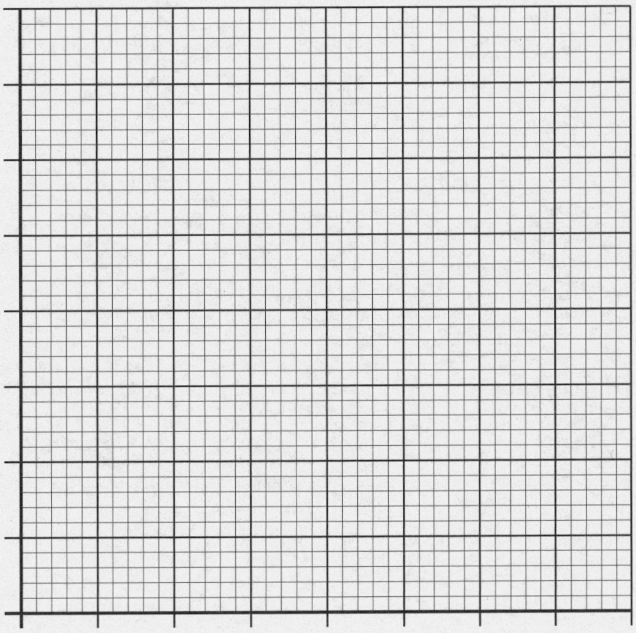

Acknowledgements

Leckie and Leckie is grateful to the copyright holders, as credited, for permission to use their material.

The following companies have very generously given permission to reproduce their copyright material free of charge: BMW(UK) Ltd for an illustration of a BMW car (2007 Credit paper p 18).